Living with Stress

A Guide for Ministers
and Church Leaders

Sarah Horsman

Foreword by Una Kroll

LUTTERWORTH PRESS
CAMBRIDGE

Lutterworth Press
P.O. Box 60
Cambridge CB1 2NT

British Library Cataloguing in Publication Data

Horsman, Sarah
  Living with stress.
  1. Christian church. Clergy. Stress
  I. Title
  253'.2

ISBN 0-7188-2772-4

Cover photograph © Derek Harris 1989

First published 1989 by Lutterworth Press

Printed and bound in Great Britain by
The Guernsey Press Co. Ltd., Guernsey, Channel Islands.

FOREWORD

I am one of the people for whom this book has been written - a Christian minister and a caring professional with a full blown 'caring personality'; a need to be needed, a habitual tendency to take on too much work, some ingrained guilt at being more fortunate and privileged than many of the people I care for, and a belief that God has called me to a way of life which involves sacrificial love.

For much of my life I have thought of stress as a challenge to be overcome by stealth. The lurking pride in that statement did not really catch up with me until I suddenly and unexpectedly erupted with anger over a trivial incident at work one day. On that day I realised that stress was no longer a challenge; it had become a problem. It took me some while to understand what had led me to that public outburst, and even longer to deal with some of the factors inside myself which were contributing to my inability either to avoid getting stressed or to cope with the unavoidable strains of a caring professional life.

Dr Sarah Horsman's book would have helped me to understand both the stress and myself had it been available to me at the time I needed it. It is scientific without being full of jargon, analytic without being intrusive, and practical without being prescriptive. Best of all, I found myself able to argue with some of the things she said without being irritated by the way she said them. She often speaks from the perspective of someone who sees the mistakes of other people more easily, perhaps, than they do themselves; yet she is able to leave that person free to select a possible solution to the problem from a number of different options. That is a rare gift. It is for this reason that I hope her book will be widely read.

Una Kroll
Deaconess Doctor

With love to Carl
and members of the Family
at the Church Army Sheldon Centre

All royalties on this book are being paid to
the Society of Mary and Martha.

CONTENTS

INTRODUCTION

I have written 'Living with Stress' while working as a member of the Society of Mary and Martha (see Appendix I). The basic information about stress-management will be of use to anyone under stress, although it has been set firmly in the context of the christian ministry. The term 'minister' is used for simplicity to refer to anyone in christian ministry whether male or female, ordained or lay, and of any denomination.

The book does not offer simplistic, universal solutions to the problem of stress, because there are none. We each have to find the solutions which work for us, and this book offers ground-rules, suggestions and ideas to enable you to find your own answers. I am enormously grateful to Captain Carl Lee, founder of the Society of Mary and Martha, for teaching me so much about people, and for repeatedly returning me from the realms of theorising to the messy but rewarding realities of life.

The first few chapters contain basic information as to how we function under stress, drawn from original research-papers and books in various fields. I am indebted to Dr Peter Nixon for introducing me to the concepts of exhaustion and human function. I would not have thought it necessary to write 'another book on stress' except that so much of what I learnt is not widely known, yet has profound implications for health. Many popular paperbacks offer simplistic solutions to the problem. Even doctors enlightened enough to recognise stress as a source of illness, often give a prescription to 'avoid too much stress' or 'go away and take it easy'. What does that mean? Usually, anxiety about being under stress is thereby added to the existing problems, with no idea of what to do about it.

To make my book readable, I have not set it out in the style of a medical journal, weighing the pros and cons of each argument and going into detail on biochemical processes. I simply offer conclusions based on in-depth research, but I would be happy to provide anyone interested with further references.[1]

1

WHAT IS THE PROBLEM?

'Stress' gets a lot of airspace these days. Everyone seems to be either suffering from it or saying that they enjoy it. Are dying from it, or saying that they could not live without it! Is there more of it about? If so, why? Or is it just a new name for an old problem? How much of a problem is it within the church? How do we recognise signs of stress in ourselves and others? Where does stress come from? And what does it do? Is everyone vulnerable to it, or just certain types of people?

Here are four fictional examples of the sort of situations which can arise. They are drawn from the experiences of real people, and reflect aspects which are not that uncommon. They demonstrate situations which cause distress and suffering to those involved, and impose a considerable drain on the churches' resources.

Mark was ordained in his early twenties, and has looked after four parishes in addition to a full-time diocesan job during the last twelve years. He is married with three grown-up children; he does not smoke, seldom drinks and eats a sensible diet. Last year he had a major heart attack, which nearly killed him. It came as a huge relief. For six years he had been struggling against the odds to do the diocesan job, as well as look after the local churches. He had been on drug treatment for two years, suffering with palpitations. Several times he had asked his immediate superiors for help as he knew that he was not coping well. He was moved to a new group of churches in the hope of a lighter workload. However, the problems moved with him, and his superiors either chose to do nothing further, or did not know what to do. Mark has now retired early (in his early fifties), on grounds of disability. He has been left a semi-invalid - more through fear than through actual damage to his heart. The church has lost ten years' service from a caring and dedicated man.

Joan is a minister's wife in her late fifties. She always shared fully in her husband's ministry as well as bringing up a family of five. Over the last three years her husband has had two lengthy periods of illness, when she nursed him for several months and carried some of the parish responsibilities. She felt exhausted for about four months. Facing each day became a huge effort, and simply meeting people drained her of her energy. She regularly returned from Sunday services completely worn out. Then she collapsed while visiting friends, and for a week barely had the strength to get out of bed. She knew the problem, and it came as something of a relief when she could no longer keep up the physical effort of carrying on. However, because she could not prove her illness with the name of a 'bug' or a doctor's prescription, the congregation did not give her 'permission' to be ill. The subtle accusation that she was malingering delayed her recovery. Joan was lucky to have avoided a serious illness, and have the chance to take stock before it was too late.

Simon is only in his late thirties, with two small children and a busy urban parish. He has two jobs. One is to be an old-fashioned 'vicar does everything' vicar, staving off financial ruin until next year, and keeping everything ticking along just as it has always been done. His other job is to bring new life and vision to the same parish - to promote individual spiritual growth, to encourage lay people to take more leadership responsibilities, and to lead the church to become more outward-looking and concerned with the local community. He does not feel able to do all that is expected of him and the strain is beginning to show in his health; he has frequent time off for minor infections, which take longer and longer to clear. Most of the time he feels 'under par'. Simon's energy and talent are being stifled and wasted; he is heading for a major physical or mental breakdown. However, it is difficult for him to find support as he is generally seen as a trouble-maker and blamed for bringing the stress upon himself. At the moment there seems to be no escape.

Mary is also in her thirties, and has experienced a great deal of distress during the early years of her ministry. Being unmarried, and working with a colleague who made no secret of his disagreement with the ordination of women, she found life extremely lonely. Her congregation was kind enough in many ways, but very little care was taken over her housing and other practical details, and she made few real friends locally. Her aims and ideals for the church turned out to be very different from those of most of the congregation. After four years she had a major 'nervous breakdown' and left the ministry altogether. While she recovered, she took various secular jobs, but it was four years before she felt able to return to the ministry. She is now proving to be a very able and caring minister in her new situation.

The problems do not just arise with people who were unstable in the first place, or should never have been accepted into the ministry. It is often the most energetic and pastorally effective men and women who get into trouble. Problems include physical illness, mental or emotional breakdown, breakdown in relationships within the family and the community, or breakdowns in social functioning (such as drinking or sexual indiscretion). In a way, the ones who get a physical illness are the lucky ones. It is socially acceptable to be ill - as long as it does not go on for too long! Most of the church, as well as society at large, does not find it at all acceptable for ministers to break down in any of the other areas. If problems arise, they are even less likely to seek help before it is too late because of the extra pressures of such censure.

Stress and sacrifice
Christians down the centuries have prayed the prayer of Saint Ignatius:

> Teach us good Lord
> To serve Thee as thou deservest;
> To give and not to count the cost;
> To fight and not to heed the wounds;
> To toil and not to seek for rest;
> To labour and not to ask for any reward,
> Save that of knowing that we do thy will,
> Through Jesus Christ, our Lord.

Many through the years have sought to live self-sacrificing lives of service as many do today. We have been brought up in a christian tradition and culture which regards self-sacrifice as a great virtue. But what is a sacrificial life? On the surface it does not tie in with modern ideas about protecting ourselves from the effects of stress. But if we believe in a God who loves us very tenderly as his children, do we at the same time believe that he expects us to 'burn out' in his service? If we do, then this has major implications for the church in providing care and resources for people who do not manage to cope. It is hardly a good example of a caring church to treat its own employees worse than many secular industries do.

On the other hand, there are very few ministers who would want to cushion themselves so effectively from stress that they no longer have any cutting edge. For many people, ministry is really about getting alongside people in distress, sharing with them in their pain and suffering. Being more detached would make life a lot more comfortable, but they would no longer be fulfilling their God-given calling. Perhaps part of the answer lies in this very fact: suffering with people is part of the calling. But so much stress appears to be not suffering *with* people, but suffering *because* of them: a subtle but important distinction!

Where do we start?
There are points of balance to be sought between the extremes of total neglect and disregard for one's own needs, and a self-centredness through which God must find it very hard to channel his love. But perhaps it is less of an 'either/or' situation than it first appears. 'Love the Lord your God with all your heart, with all your soul, with all your mind and with all your strength. . . . Love your neighbour as yourself.' The Great Commandment summarises the starting-point from which we must work: love of God is first and foremost. Without a yearning for him, a seeking daily to walk more closely with him, all the techniques of stress-management become so much hot air. However - and perhaps because of this - problems of stress are often seen as spiritual failure. The prescription given is to pray harder. But there are times when this is not the answer, because the problem is not a spiritual one. Godly men and women

do end up in difficulties, which simply do not get resolved by praying harder. The second part of the commandment is to love your neighbour *as yourself*. With no love (or respect) for self, with no understanding of our own individual worth and preciousness in the sight of God, how can we begin to love our neighbour? A deeper knowledge of ourselves, what makes us tick, what our strengths and weaknesses are, is a foundation-stone on which to build an effective ministry. People who live in certain ways run the risk of getting ill, whether they are Christian ministers or mafia bosses. God does not seem to offer immunity for those who abuse themselves in the service of his kingdom. There are times when he can, and does, miraculously intervene. But we have been created in such a way that, if we follow the ground-rules, our bodies and minds will normally give good service. We are fortunate enough to live in an age when much ancient wisdom is being confirmed by scientific research. This book draws on both modern facts and ancient wisdom to present coherent and workable ideas for living more effectively with stress, to which we now turn.

2

WHAT IS STRESS?

Most people will understand what is meant when you say that you find a person, a task, or a particular situation, stressful. The concept is of something that arouses tension, anxiety and a certain set of short-term physical and mental responses. If you tell someone that you are 'under stress' or 'finding life stressful at the moment' you are implying that things are getting you down on a rather longer-term basis; that life is becoming more of a struggle than an enjoyment. But one of the problems with the concept of stress is that the word has come to be used so widely that it can end up meaning next to nothing.

Stress can mean both the positive experience of stimulation and challenge, and the negative long-term one of distress and exhaustion; the external, provoking situation (stressor), and the internal physical, cognitive, emotional and behavioural responses. I use the term for the basic short-term stress response and for the negative long-term experience, but not for the experience of challenge and stimulation. Some writers try to differentiate clearly between the 'stressor' and the 'stress response'. As the two are so intimately related I find it more helpful to use 'stress' rather loosely, to include both aspects. Stress in real life is neither entirely from without, nor entirely from within. Some situations are so difficult that almost anyone would experience stress, while others are so congenial that very few would. But the degree of stress experienced is very dependent on the individual and his experiences, resources and coping abilities. Researchers who try to measure stress face many of the same problems as people measuring pain. Because we are dealing with all the complexities of human experience, any attempt will be at best a crude indicator.

This next section will help you to recognise stress both in yourself and in others. The bodily symptoms can be quite powerful, and because they overlap with symptoms of specific illnesses they can be frightening. Fear then compounds with anxiety, and so the stress-cycle gets worse. Some of the emotional, cognitive and behavioural responses can equally be mistaken for instability, incompetence or laziness, but instructions to 'pull your socks up', or 'snap out of it', are not helpful to someone under stress. Far more sympathetic and constructive help can be offered when you understand what is going on.

Short-term stress
Short-term stress is the body's way of providing extra energy to deal with an emergency - the primitive 'fight or flight' reaction. You will probably recognise some or all of the following symptoms:

fast heart beat	fast breathing
heart palpitations	tight stomach
racing thoughts	feeling sick
faintness	diarrhoea
flushing	trembling
cold hands and feet	sweaty palms
tense muscles	dry mouth
desire to pass water	'butterflies'
shortness of breath	feeling anxious

In response to a threatening situation, adrenaline is secreted into the blood stream which prepares the body for physical exertion. It is this response which enables people to perform amazing feats, like lifting a car off a trapped child which they could not possibly do in cold blood. Short-term stress is not normally damaging to the body because once the threat has gone you relax and the body's chemistry returns to normal.

Long-term stress
Long-term stress is a sign that repeated demands for short-term boosting have eventually used up the body's reserves. Perhaps you recognise some of these symptoms:

muscle tension	muddled thinking
general aches and pains	forgetfulness
irritability	loss of creativity
feeling bogged down in details	indecision
headaches	loss of drive and willpower
loss of creative vision	sleeplessness
aches and pains	tiredness not relieved by sleep
loss of enthusiasm	indigestion
cynicism	loss of energy
loss of appetite	tearfulness
frustration	loss of interest in sex
loss of perspective	general slowing down
poor judgment	repeated colds/infections

Chapter four below gives more detail on how we manage to get ourselves into such a state. The message for the moment is:

1. You are not alone; many others get into this condition, often not realising that these are signs of stress.

2. It is not the end of the line; the symptoms are warning signs that you need to be asking what the causes are and finding out what can be done.

Burnout

'Burnout' is an American term with rather emotive connotations. It basically refers to a state of physical, emotional and mental exhaustion that results from long-term involvement with people in emotionally demanding situations. Symptoms are those of long-term stress, plus:

stereotyped behaviour	blaming 'clients'
emotional deadness	withdrawal from colleagues
loss of interest in 'clients'	loss of meaning

I will use 'burnout' to refer to research which uses this terminology, but personally I do not think that it is a useful expression.

Mind and body

The experience of emotion is intimately linked with electrical activity within the brain, which enables our emotional experiences

8

to cause changes in our physical state. Emotional experience such as anxiety, elation or fear sets off a particular pattern of electrical activity in the brain. Nerve cells in one particular region, the hypothalamus, secrete hormones when they are stimulated, which send messages to its neighbour, the pituitary gland, to produce other hormones. These then travel round the body in the blood stream, some of them acting directly, others giving coded messages to other glands to produce further hormones.

A hormone is a body chemical which carries messages around the body in the blood stream. (If the nervous system be compared to the telephone network, the hormonal system may be likened to the postal network.) Hormones instruct body cells on many vital functions, such as digesting food, growth, healing and reproduction.

Some suggest that all emotions cause a stereotyped outpouring of hormones, including adrenaline. According to this theory the effect on the body is the same; it does not matter whether the experience is essentially a happy one or a distressing one. This leads to the conclusion that all strong emotions, whether exciting or upsetting, are to be avoided. The theory has arisen through having to use very blunt instruments to examine a very delicate system. A newer, and I feel a more promising, theory is that each emotion has its own unique hormonal 'thumbprint'. This means that although anger and joy may both cause adrenaline to be released, they will have very different effects on the body. Looking at patterns in this way, rather than simply measuring individual hormones, will probably help to shed more light in this area.

Important hormones
Two important stress hormones which have been well studied are adrenaline and cortisol. More research will help us to understand the role of others more fully.

Adrenaline and its sister hormone noradrenaline are together referred to as the catecholamines. Their chemical structure and effects are similar, and both are produced by the adrenal glands (one is attached to the top of each kidney). Together they are the main hormones responsible for the 'fight or flight' reaction. Sugar and fat are released into the blood stream to make emergency energy available for muscular effort. They also have powerful effects on the constriction and dilation of the blood vessels; they raise the blood pressure and divert blood away from the internal organs towards the muscles, to prepare the body for physical action.

Situations of challenge and effort are particularly effective in raising the catecholamine levels. The more intense the emotional experience, the higher the levels, to the extent that intense challenge and effort can raise blood levels almost as high as those found in a tumour of the adrenal gland (known as phaeochromocytoma). I have known at least one minister end up in hospital being investigated for a phaeochromocytoma, because neither he nor his doctors realised that his trouble was severe stress. The good news is that levels can be significantly reduced by situations which evoke feelings of calmness and equanimity.

Cortisol is involved in a variety of routine activities such as the regulation of fat, sugar and protein metabolism, maintenance of the balance of salt and water, and control of the immune system. It is also known to speed up hardening of the arteries.

It has long been believed that cortisol helps confer increased resistance to stress, but this appears to conflict with the fact that at high levels it suppresses the immune system. This leaves the individual 'immune compromised', that is, more vulnerable to things like infection, cancers and auto-immune diseases (when the immune system starts to damage one's own body). One possible explanation is that cortisol is protecting the body against some of its own over-zealous reactions to stress, rather than against stress *per se*. Either way, it is a hormone with powerful effects. Situations that produce feelings of distress, defeat and despair are the ones which most effectively raise the level of cortisol, while feelings of contentedness and well-being bring the levels down to below normal.

3

STRESS AND HEALTH

According to the World Health Organisation, health is not merely the absence of disease but a state of physical, mental and social well-being. Using this definition, it is obvious that stress can cause ill health. We all know that, when under stress, we are not in a state of total well-being. But does stress also cause ill health in the narrower definition of specific disease states, measurable in the laboratory? To answer this question it is useful to look first at how the body maintains health.

Maintaining internal order
In order to survive, all living creatures need to make sure that conditions within the body stay within closely defined limits, regardless of what is happening in their environment. The maintenance of order within the body is called homeostasis, and most of the time this is achieved by complex systems of 'negative feedback' control.

In negative feedback systems there is a continual oscillation about the correct level, with departures from the norm in either direction being rapidly corrected. But negative feedback systems themselves can only work within a certain range of conditions. Outside this range the system cannot cope, and 'positive feedback' sets in which escalates the problem. When the conditions become too extreme, vital body processes cannot take place properly, and so illness (and eventually death) occur.

This basic pattern of feedback control is used for the maintenance of many body functions such as blood pressure; blood-sugar, fat and protein; as well as the salt, water and acid content of the body. Once the regulating system is pushed beyond its capacity to cope there is a breakdown in function.

So we have a whole network of finely balanced systems

designed to maintain the mechanics of body function. The spanner in the works is that in responding to emotional experiences, we release more of the same hormones that control these delicate systems. The changes induced by emotion can be sufficiently powerful to override regularly the feedback controls which try to restore homeostasis. The effects of the mind over the body are indeed very powerful, and the signs and symptoms of long-term stress are warnings that the body is not coping with the assault.

Mind and body
Often the term 'psychosomatic' illness is used in a rather pejorative way, and confused with malingering or hypochondria. Malingering is feigning illness when you know you are not ill; the hypochondriac sincerely believes that he is ill when there is no physical sign of it. A psychosomatic illness is a real physical illness, caused by this disruption of body processes by means of the powerful effects of our emotional experiences. Because so many physical causes of illness - bacteria, viruses, parasites, etc - have been discovered in the last century, and many powerful therapeutic drugs developed, we have slipped into the trap of thinking of illness in purely physical terms.

Unfortunately, this mechanistic view is very prevalent, partly, at least, because the profit motive lurks behind so much of our current thinking. Pharmaceutical companies stand to make such huge profits from drugs that they can afford to spend lavishly on both research and promotion. It is clearly not in their interests to research non-drug answers. We desperately need far more 'neutral' money to be put into basic research for the benefit of everyone. In the long term, good stress management is economically essential, both for individuals and nations, but long-term investment is needed.

At one time it was thought that there were certain diseases with psychological causes, and the rest had physical causes. Now it seems more appropriate to ask what role psychological effects have in the causation of each and every disease. So often we fail to even ask the right questions: 'Why this person with this illness at this time?' and 'What is the meaning of this illness?' Holistic medicine does not mean adding care for a person's mind on to a basically unaltered care for their body. It requires a fundamentally integrated approach to the person who is mind and soul as well as body, who participates in a network of relationships and social duties. The roots of illness, and its cures, should be sought in each area.

Heart disease

With coronary heart disease there is evidence that the traditional risk factors of cigarette smoking, high blood-pressure, high blood-cholesterol and obesity, all increase the risk of illness. There is a big drive for GPs to screen their patients for high blood-pressure and high blood-cholesterol (especially middle-aged men). However, there are problems with this approach:

1. These traditional risk factors are known to 'explain' only 10-20% of coronary heart disease. We all know of slim non-smokers, who eat a good diet, take plenty of exercise, and still manage to have heart attacks.

2. If some, or all, of these factors are actually caused by stress in the first place, then treatment will be more concerned with alleviating the cause (stress) than its symptoms (the risk factors). Chapter four lists some of the physical changes which can be measured in people who are exhausted; they include many heart disease risk factors.

Friedman and Rosenman[1] were the first to introduce the idea of the 'Type A' personality of someone who is competitive, achievement oriented and restless with a sense of urgency. This was found to predict heart disease better than blood-cholesterol levels, and only slightly less well than diastolic blood pressure. 'Personality' was changed to 'behaviour' when it was found that those who changed their behaviour after a heart attack were less likely to have another than those who did not. There are many other research findings which provide evidence of the mind-body link, they include:

1. People who, in addition to being driven to make great efforts are also depressed and perceive themselves as helpless and lacking social support, are especially vulnerable to coronary heart disease.

13

2. Those who perceive their partners to be unsupportive are more likely to have heart disease than those who see them as constantly supportive.

3. Hard work, unfavourable life-events and 'Type A' behaviour, all show a relationship with raised blood-pressure and raised blood-cholesterol.

These findings obviously have important implications for the prevention and treatment of heart disease which is now responsible for 50% of deaths under sixty years of age in the western world. Although not backed by firm evidence, the impression of the Society of Mary and Martha is that heart disease is especially common among Christian ministers. Perhaps this is not surprising, given that the heart does not just pump blood round the body but actually provides for the 'effort of living'.

People at risk

Totman[2] has reviewed much of the literature concerned with psychosomatic causes of disease, and feels that the so-called 'Type A' behaviour is not just associated with heart disease. Friedman and Rosenman's 'Type A' may be just one example of a wider tendency to hold rigid and/or extreme standards. Totman's theory is that people become ill when they are no longer able to cope with their social environment, either because the environment is so bad or because their coping skills are limited. He includes the following in his list of 'Type A' traits:

self-sacrificing	tendency to suppress emotions
perfectionist	rigid standards
overly-conscientious	expectations of impossibly high
strong sense of duty	standards of achievement
tightly self-controlled	priority placed on doing the
obsessive	socially accepted thing

According to Totman's theory, these traits reduce people's ability to adapt to a changing social environment. Some of them may well be admirable qualities - as with a sense of duty, self-control and self-sacrifice - but it is important to look at the motivation behind these qualities: Is it really a duty to a loving and compassionate God, or to the expectations of society or the congregation? Is it self-control understood as the ability to avoid silly emotional outbursts in inappropriate situations, or the avoidance of any emotional expression? Does it demonstrate self-sacrifice, following Christ's example of obedience to his Father's will, or a refusal to listen to one's own God-given needs?

Individuals at high risk of illness have also been described in terms of their predominant mental and emotional states, and in terms of their relationships with the social environment. Totman again draws out the major themes from a large number of researchers:

deep seated sense of frustration	helplessness - the 'giving up' reaction
dissatisfaction with work or life in general	alienation from society
self-depreciation and feelings of failure	status incongruity (moved up or down the social scale)
absence of self-esteem	role ambiguity (unclear what is expected of them)
resentment	
depression and anxiety	cultural mobility

living in an environment which is:

unpredictable or undergoing rapid change	lacking social cohesion and social support

Unfortunately, research into this sort of question often cannot give clear-cut answers. Because of the methodological and ethical difficulties encountered, it is probably impossible to 'prove' a case in the truly rigorous, scientific sense. However, when many studies from different fields combine to point in roughly the same direction, I feel that it is well worth our taking notice. Especially in this case, when scriptural wisdom is being confirmed by modern research. The only reason some of it seems new and strange is that for a couple of generations we thought that the age of the magic pill had superseded the ancient wisdom. It has not!

Life-events

The importance of 'life-events' is often mentioned in the context of stress-control and illness. Much has been made of research suggesting that one can total up a 'life-events' score' for the last year, and thence predict the likelihood of falling ill over the next year. The original work was carried out by Holmes and Rahe [3] who compiled a list of life-events (the schedule of recent experience, SRE) such as marriage, birth of a child, prison term, financial difficulties, or relationship problems. Events which appear positive and enjoyable are included as well as the negative ones. Each was assigned a score according to the amount of adjustment required by a person facing that event. From using the SRE with various groups of people, mainly naval recruits, it was concluded that the risk of illness increased with high SRE scores. Many popular books use adaptations of the SRE for people to work out their own stress scores.

However, this research can be interpreted in other ways, and it is possible that a high life-events' score leads to 'treatment seeking behaviour', such as seeing a doctor, rather than necessarily to actual illness. Perhaps under stress they were seeking the human support they needed? Or perhaps they were interpreting body symptoms in a different light when feeling stressed? I mention this to caution against taking some of the popular 'solutions' at face value, but it would be rash to throw the baby out along with the bath-water. Change can be a stressor but it is really the emotional experience accompanying the change which matters.

Hardiness

Hardiness is a person's resistance to becoming ill when faced with stressful life-events,[4] and includes the following qualities:

1. Commitment, i.e. the disposition to be active and involved in events rather than withdrawn and passive. It involves saying a wholehearted 'yes' to some activities, and 'no' to others.

2. Control, i.e. the tendency to feel and act as if you have influence to change at least some aspects of your environment.

3. Challenge, i.e. the belief that change is interesting and an incentive to growth and development, and not a threat to security.

Efforts should be made to reduce unnecessary stresses of change, but the experience of stress, and its effects on our minds and bodies, can be altered by our outlook and coping skills. This book will help you develop the skills which will be useful for you.

16

BODY MANAGEMENT

Distress and effort

The combination of distress and effort involves raising the levels of both adrenaline and cortisol which are potentially dangerous to the body. Figure 1 represents the 'danger quadrant' of combined effort and distress, and the relaxation and wellbeing which can counterbalance them.

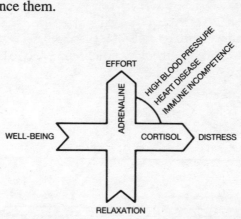

Figure 1. The danger quadrant.[1]

To move out of the danger quadrant you need to find ways of either reducing the intensity of the effort and distress, or counterbalancing their effects with extra relaxation and feelings of wellbeing. This is an important concept, because so often people are merely told to 'avoid stress'. The body is surprisingly resilient to hard work (effort) when you are in a positive frame of mind, but effort combined with emotional distress can be damaging. If neither the effort nor the distress can be altered very much (at least for the time being), then you will need to find ways of relaxing which suit you in order to bring the adrenaline levels down. Things that promote wellbeing (and reduce those cortisol levels) are even more individual, and would include such things as friendships, hobbies, achievement, making love, being creative, etc.

There are no universal prescriptions for reducing stress; we each need to know what works for us as individuals. The effort-and-distress axis is a useful tool in finding the right balance for you. Finding the balance also involves recognising the warning signs of long-term stress or exhaustion, and relearning what it feels like to be in a positive, healthily functioning state. This knowledge would have come naturally to us once, but our culture has caused us to 'unlearn' it.

The human function curve

This has been developed by consultant cardiologist Dr Peter Nixon to explain the concept of healthy functioning and exhaustion:

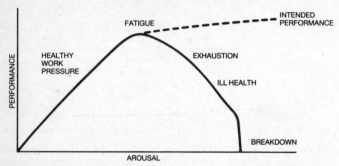

Figure 2. The human function curve.[2]

'Arousal' is the degree of stimulation or effort involved in doing a task; 'performance' is the measure of success in doing it. In the 'healthy work pressure' part of the curve we are functioning at our best. As Nixon puts it, 'the healthy individual working on the upslope has rapid, adaptable thought, comes up with original intuitive solutions, is vigorous, can take on extra problems without a shift in pace, and can maintain sustained effort.' What better description of the state in which we should all like to be! However, our bodies do have limits, and there comes the point of fatigue where further arousal (effort) no longer has the desired effect of improving performance. The homeostatic mechanisms simply cannot maintain internal order with this degree of pressure and disruption, and you go 'over the top' of the curve, into the downslope of exhaustion. Problems which can arise at this stage include:

high blood-pressure } known risk factors for coronary heart
high blood-cholesterol } disease
faster blood clotting - increases risk of stroke and heart attacks
high blood-sugar - increases risk of diabetes
water retention - feelings of lethargy and swelling
high blood uric acid - found in gout
immune incompetence - reduced resistance to infection, plus increased risk of cancer

We all come into the world with different bank balances, in terms of body reserves and resilience. In other words, the height of the human function curve is different for each of us. Some people can violate their bodies for many years before it catches up with them; for others the day of reckoning comes much sooner.

Exhaustion

Either way, once in the exhaustion phase, you are faced with a new and unfamiliar set of rules. The goal-posts have been moved without you realising it. During healthy function, when you wanted to perform better, you simply had to try harder. But when you are exhausted, trying harder simply pushes you further down the downslope of exhaustion; you are less able to cope, and more at risk of ill health. The dotted line represents the desired performance you are trying to achieve, which becomes further and further out of reach. The further you fall short of this intended performance, the more distressed and inadequate you feel. The vicious circle is only broken by the opportunity for rest and recuperation, either taken by choice, or enforced by illness or breakdown. Nixon observes that it takes on average about two years from 'going over the top' at the point of fatigue to the point of a serious breakdown in health.

The exhausted state is characterised by:
increasingly obsessional and pedantic behaviour, bad temper and aggressive responses. The ability to discriminate between essential and non-essential matters is lost. Long-term aims vanish in an exasperated bogging down in details. Longer hours are worked but less is achieved. . . . In the attempt to maintain performance, despite fatigue, there is an increasing use of stimulants and an invasion of the hours for sleeping and family leisure by work.[3]

Nixon teaches his patients that symptoms are for listening to in the process of learning to live with the strengths and limitations of our bodies. The drug industry has successfully convinced us that there is a pill for every ill, that symptoms only require suppressing with drugs. But if your headache, sleeplessness or indigestion is being caused by stress, taking pills may reduce the discomfort, but they do not address the cause. Masking the warning symptoms allows you to go on abusing your body until something worse happens. It is not always wrong to take a pain-killer or a sleeping tablet, but if you find yourself needing them regularly, it is time to take stock and see what needs changing in your lifestyle.

A checklist is used at Charing Cross with people trying to discover why they have ended up on the downslope:
Because too much is demanded of me?
Because I cannot say 'no' when I should?
Because I am not sufficiently in control? Cannot cope?
Too angry, too tense, too upset, too irritable, too indignant?
Too many people-hassles?
Too many time pressures? Too impatient?
Because I am not sleeping *well* enough to keep well?
Because I am not keeping fit enough to stay well?
Because I am not balancing periods of hard effort with adequate sleep and relaxation?
Because I am out of real energy and using sheer willpower to keep going?
Because I am infallible, indispensable, immortal and indestructible?
Recovery to healthy functioning can only come through a period of complete rest, and then learning to stay on the healthy upslope.

Adequate sleep and rest are important, as well as control of arousal levels by anxiety and tension reducing techniques. People are taught how to breathe properly, and how to exercise safely and well. Most important of all, perhaps, is the rebuilding of self-esteem: teaching people that they do have a say in how they run their lives, that they are valuable as people, and that life does have meaning and purpose. It is sad that the church should be having to look to the secular world to relearn such a fundamental part of our Christian faith.

Overbreathing

Breathing appears to be the most natural thing we do, but as many as one person in ten habitually overbreathes (hyperventilates). The popular image is of neurotic women who hysterically gasp for breath, but it is usually much more subtle. Men and women are equally susceptible to overbreathing, and many do it for years without anyone realising.

The symptoms of overbreathing are vague and varied, so that many people get labelled neurotic and trail round seeing different specialists. The list of possible symptoms is a long one, but here are some of the more common ones:

cramps	pins and needles
muscle aches and pains	numbness
trembling	dizziness
tension	visual disturbance
anxiety	headaches
feelings of unreality	palpitations
weakness	rapid heart beat
tiredness	chest pain
sleep disturbance	angina
breathlessness	

The trouble is that you do not have to over breathe by very much to suffer the consequences. Breathing is an automatic function of the body, but it is also under conscious control, which is vital if you want to go swimming, play a musical instrument, or even just hold a conversation. The respiratory centre in the brain is set to keep the carbon dioxide content of the blood at a steady level, and the kidney is set to maintain the acidity of the blood. Breathing too much air does not increase the level of blood oxygen, but it does lower the carbon dioxide level, making the blood less acid. The kidney objects to this, and excretes some bicarbonate (dissolved carbon dioxide, which is an alkali) into the urine to raise the blood acidity to normal. The kidney's preference overrides the respiratory centre, which then has to settle for the new lower level of blood carbon dioxide. After a while it resets its 'thermostat' and accepts this abnormally low level as the normal one.

All this would not matter, except that a low blood carbon dioxide causes the unpleasant symptoms outlined above. Many of them are a nuisance in their own right, but they also mimic heart disease and other serious illness. People who overbreathe all day, every day, even by only a small amount, are living with a carbon dioxide level very near the threshold for symptoms to occur. It may then take only a small trigger, such as a lively conversation or physical exertion, to reduce the level that little bit further and trigger the symptoms.

To find out if you overbreathe, lie down on the floor and place a book on your tummy and another on your chest. The book on the tummy should move up and down, but the one on the chest should stay still. (Tummy breathing is, in fact, using the diaphragm, while chest breathing is using the muscles between the ribs.) If you breathe with your chest (ie overbreathe) your family and friends may notice that you take deep breaths or sigh a lot. Many people believe that it is more correct to breathe with the chest than the tummy, and may have been told to 'take deep breaths' if they are feeling anxious or tense. But breathing with the chest is primarily a cultural thing, linked with the heaving bosom of the sexually attractive woman, or the puffed-out chest of a virile man! People may start chest breathing during singing training, army drill, from wearing tight-waisted garments, or because of pain after an abdominal operation. You only have to do it for a few weeks for your 'thermostat' to be reset, and the habit become well and truly fixed. Fortunately, it is only a habit, and can be unlearnt with a little patience. (Retraining your breathing is outlined in Appendix 1.) We only need to breathe with the upper chest when there is a genuine need for increased oxygen supply to the body, which occurs during physical exercise.

It is very useful for everyone to keep an eye on their breathing at times of stress and anxiety, because of the vicious circle whereby overbreathing causes adrenaline production which, in turn, causes further overbreathing. Adrenaline encourages breathing with the chest because this is what is needed for extra oxygen supply for physical 'fight or flight'. But like the other effects of adrenaline, it is a damaging response when there is emotional distress but no physical exertion.

Some of the most powerful triggers to overbreathing are thought to be loss (eg bereavement or failure), separation, and impotent anger. Even people who do not habitually overbreathe will tend to do so in these stressful situations. Learning to focus on your breathing, and keep it coming from the tummy, is an excellent aid to keeping your adrenaline low and your head cool in these circumstances.

Public speaking is a stressful situation for many people, and one which is particularly good at upsetting the breathing pattern and causing breathlessness. Mastering the art of tummy breathing will help in this situation as well. A few minutes of quiet breathing is also a very good preparation for relaxation, prayer or meditation, as it helps to still the body and the mind.

The key message from this chapter is that our bodies provide us with valuable information - if we can learn the language. Culturally, we have lost awareness of what exhaustion is, and we are no longer tuned-in to the warning signals. It is well worth relearning these ground rules in order to make the most of life: 'For best results, follow the maker's instructions.'

Chronic
Air swallowing is
a problem too: causing
Excess wind) as
unpleasant sensations

5

STRESSES OF THE JOB

There is no doubt that the job of a minister has many inherent stresses; some of them are shared with many other jobs, others are specific to it.

Availability
One of the stresses most often commented on is the twenty-four hour availability. Most 'helping professionals' these days have a buffer between them and the outside world, in the form of a receptionist or secretary. At the end of the day they leave their place of work and go home, where they are not normally accessible to clients. By contrast, a minister is often the first port of call for everything from the most trivial administrative or practical matters, to pastoral care in an emotionally charged emergency. Even on a day off or at home in the evening, it is more than likely that he will be called upon for something.

This issue of availability ties in with two other areas - living up to the expectations of others, and the time-pressures consequential to a heavy workload. Ministers are generally expected to exude an air of serene goodness, expressed in a willingness to help anyone, at any time. Woe betide the minister who loses his cool, whether with an individual or at a church committee meeting! Many people simply do not realise what a heavy workload ministers carry. However light-heartedly meant, the joke about only working one day a week does not go down well.

Risk factors
How many items on this list of job stresses do you recognise as your own?

24

feeling out of control of the workload

being bored

simultaneous demands being made

pressure of time

lack of meaning in work

lack of opportunity to learn and develop

lack of structure within which to work

lack of positive feedback, or any feedback at all

cramped or noisy work-environment

large numbers of people needing help

people with very difficult problems

poor relationships with colleagues

lack of challenge

excess paperwork and red-tape

lack of communication with superiors

policy influenced by uninformed outsiders

role conflict (several different things expected)

role ambiguity (unclear as to what is expected)

lack of opportunity for creativity and innovation

little variety of work

lack of work evaluation

This list is drawn from research into secular job situations among the helping professions,[1] but it is striking how many of the items regularly crop up when talking with ministers. The items on the list have all been correlated with high staff burnout in secular jobs, and it is high time we started taking them a lot more seriously within the church, especially when looking at preventative physical and mental health-care of our ministers. Some of them are items which can be tackled by the individual, but others do require more fundamental restructuring at a higher level.

Workload

When it comes to workload, the simple fact is that there is always more work to be done than there is time in which to do it. The work is potentially never ending, and it is never possible to put your feet up at the end of the day and say, 'I've finished'. This of itself is a difficult situation, but add a pinch of justification by works, a dose of self-criticism, a smattering of guilt, a hint of fear of failure, and problems start to loom large. This is one example where the job is itself difficult but the problems can be compounded by internal pressures.

25

Here are some ideas for approaching the issue of workload:

1. Be satisfied with an honest day's work, and do not take to bed heaps of guilt for not doing what cannot be done. Some people simply do not know what they should reasonably expect of themselves, and think that they are slacking when in reality they are working like a Trojan. This seems to be a particular problem for people entering the ministry late in life, perhaps after becoming accustomed to a more defined routine. Special care needs to be taken of these people, as they adapt to a totally new routine, often without guidelines.

2. Keep a rough tally of the number of hours worked each week. This need not be a rigid 'down tools' when the hours are up, but it is a useful check for making sure that things are not getting out of hand. Somewhere between 45 and 60 hours a week is a reasonable level at which to aim. One minister who aims for an average of 55 hours a week finds that if he works much more '... I lose the ability to think creatively, my thoughts become stale, my sermons become boring, people become irritations to me, I behave unreasonably towards my children, plus physical things like headaches ....' This is a good illustration of what I mean by learning to be aware of yourself. 55 hours is not a magic number; some will work more, and others less. What is important is to listen in this way to what *you* are able to cope with. Another minister regularly worked 85 hours or more for many years but, following a nervous breakdown, looks back with regret. He feels that at most he was only actually achieving the equivalent of 70 hours' work because he was too tired to work effectively, and is sad at not having spent all those wasted hours on something more creative.

3. Work out your priorities, both on a day-to-day basis, and with regard to longer-term objectives. One of the symptoms of long-term stress is getting bogged down with everyday things, losing the ability to look ahead and plan sensibly. Do talk through your priorities regularly with a sympathetic colleague or superior if you can. Having a second perspective can help iron out problems at an early stage. On a day-to-day basis it may be a case of spending ten minutes first thing listing what has to be done and putting them in order of priority. For an extra boost, write down a

few things you have already done, so you can grandly cross them off!

4. Could some of the work be done by someone else? True, it can sometimes be quicker to do it yourself in the short run (and if you are like me you will firmly believe that you are the only person who can do it properly anyway!) but the price of isolationism is too high. It can be very humbling for an ill workaholic to see the church wheels continuing to turn: 'How dare they manage without me!' Sometimes we work too hard because we need to be needed. On the other hand, there are often very entrenched attitudes among the congregation: 'Well it's different if the *vicar* does it'. Such attitudes only get changed by time and patience.

5. *Feel* in control of the workload. Knowing that you are able to say 'no' is vital. You may not choose to say it very often, but there is all the difference in the world between feeling trapped in an unavoidable task, and knowing that you are only doing it because you have assented to do so. There are some things which it is right and proper to refuse, even if people try and make you feel guilty over it. Do not feel that you need to make excuses; the fact that you need time for yourself or your family is a good enough reason. It is all too easy to concoct bogus excuses and then ruin your hard-earned private time with fear of being found out.

Boredom

Boredom and lack of meaning in work do not appear at first sight to relate to ministry, but problems can occur with specific tasks within the job. Robin Pryor[2] quotes an Australian study in which nearly half of the responding ministers enjoyed least of all the administrative aspect of their job. In addition, a quarter of them felt they were not competent to do it. This would seem to suggest that ministers should either be given better training in administration, or released from it in favour of more people-oriented tasks.

Supervision

Supervision, evaluation and feedback form a much neglected area. The 'lone ranger' style of ministry is deeply entrenched in many church traditions, but most caring professionals these days have some means of evaluation and support as an integral part of the system within which they work. It is sad that for many people a supervisor is either someone who is always looking over their shoulder waiting to pounce when they make a mistake, or someone who is never available until things have gone wrong beyond repair.

Creative supervision is about good people-management; it includes improving a person's skills, promoting their self-esteem, and being available for consultation before a problem becomes a crisis. In secular situations it is usually recommended that the work-supervisor should be concerned with the development and functioning of the person in his work context only, and not be involved as a counsellor for personal problems. Within the church superiors are often pastorally responsible for ministers, as well as having influence over their work and future job-prospects. In this situation there is often a very genuine fear of 'black marks' being entered in the big book when ministers admit to having difficulties.

In practice, some people get appointed to higher office within the church for their academic or administrative skills rather than pastoral abilities. Also, the demands of the job may be such that even the most caring pastor may not be able to look after the large number of ministers in his care effectively. In making confidential counselling services available to ministers, it is often useful to cross geographical and denominational boundaries, as many schemes are presently doing successfully.

The availability of counselling services does not reduce the need for good basic supervisory structures within the churches. How many superiors ever get offered a good training in how to supervise? Listed below are some aspects of good work supervision correlated with low staff burnout in secular settings:[3]

1. Clear structures and information
2. Appropriate and accurate communication
3. Unambiguous expectations
4. Freedom to make decisions when appropriate
5. Encouragement of creativity and innovation
6. Opportunities to learn and improve skills
7. Regular constructive evaluation of performance
8. Gradual build-up of workload when beginning a new job

We all know what panic can be generated among students around examination or assessment time, much of which could be alleviated by clear information and unambiguous expectations. There is the suspicion that certain behaviours and attitudes are publicly encouraged, but in reality penalised.

It is often tacitly assumed that this anxiety is no bad thing as it keeps students on their toes and makes them work harder. However, it also lays poor foundations for a mature attitude to work supervision in later life. The one goal is to be free from the threat of assessment and the anxiety it generates. One colleague, with all the sensitivity of a wart hog, proclaims that examination stress is definitely a good thing because it prepares people for the stressful world of work. It does not prepare people to be members of a co-operating team, able to give and receive constructive criticism, or to care for and develop other team-members, especially juniors.

I wonder if some of the competitiveness so often found among ministers begins at these same roots of examination and assessment competition? Ministers often feel inadequate in the face of other people's successes when they get together at conferences or fraternals. Everyone then has to boost their own morale by having a few success stories up their sleeves in order to compete. How sad, when such occasions provide ideal opportunities for mutual support and encouragement! The brave ones who let down their guard and admit to finding things a bit tough are often surprised at how many others feel just the same, but had not dared to say so.

Evaluation

Evaluation is a particularly difficult task in Christian ministry. The real results of the work will only be measured in heaven, but how tempting it is to play the numbers' game here on earth! It is even more tempting in the absence of more appropriate and properly thought-out targets and goals. Targets that are too high condemn one to perpetual failure, but with low targets you run the risk of complacency and under-achievement.

A good supervision and evaluation scheme has been pioneered in the anglican diocese of Birmingham. The Barnabas Scheme offers full-time ministers, and especially those in their first incumbencies, free confidential support and consultancy in their ministry. The minister meets with his consultant two or three times a year to analyse tasks, set priorities, and evaluate what is being achieved. The focus is on areas directly concerning work. Ministers acting as consultants are themselves using some form of partnership or consultancy in their own ministry, and the initial consultancy period of three years provides a training-base to go on and provide consultancy for others. Senior members of the local church can fulfil a vital supporting role for their minister in giving constructive feedback. So often the only feedback a minister gets is of a negative nature; a little encouragement can go a long way. Other colleagues and superiors might even value your support and encouragement - you never know!

Expectations

Many ministers feel ill-prepared for the wide variety of skills which they are expected to perform competently. A minister may be called upon to be teacher, parish organiser, administrator, pastor (visiting and counselling), preacher, priest (leading worship and administering the sacraments), evangelist, theologian (studying and writing), spiritual director, and social reformer; not to mention youth group leader, carpenter, plumber, fund-raiser, reconciler, family man/woman, entertainer, and a fountain of unlimited goodness. This gives plenty of scope for role-conflict and ambiguity to arise.

Different ministers will obviously have their own unique strengths and weaknesses. It is very draining to live with the nagging suspicion that you are not doing all that is expected of you. This may very well be the case, if there are people in the congregation whose expectations and priorities are different from your own, or if they are forever comparing you with the wonderful Reverend so-and-so. Such ghosts are sometimes better laid to rest by bringing them out in the open for discussion and negotiation. One minister asked his church council to suggest how many hours a week he should be spending on certain tasks. One church warden's suggestions added up to a grand total of 160 hours a week. No wonder the poor minister felt he was not doing all that was expected of him.

Given that you can't please all the people all the time, it is important that you know what your priorities are, what you are good at, where you have room to develop, and the things that are best done by someone else. If you always take your lead from other people's expectations of you, you are condemned to fail repeatedly.

The expectations on a minister do not stop at competence in his work. His behaviour, leisure activities, friendships and family life are all considered fair game for comment and criticism. This persistent pressure can be quite intolerable for anyone trying to maintain a good image at all times. (These aspects will be discussed further in the chapters seven and eight.)

Getting involved

The last but not least of his job pressures is the minister's deep involvement in emotionally demanding situations. Many helping professionals are taught to avoid getting too involved, but part of the essence of Christian ministry is this sharing in people's suffering. How can we go about being deeply involved with people without becoming victims of long-term stress and burnout?

One of the first preventative steps is to recognise that it is indeed demanding work. It may *look* like just sitting and chatting, but being involved with people in distress is as energy consuming as being a lumberjack. When you are sharing in other people's distress, that needs to be added to your own effort and distress equation, which means allowing extra opportunities for relaxation and promotion of well-being. Once again there are no hard and fast formulae to follow, just the more difficult - and more rewarding - path of knowing yourself and knowing with what you can cope.

6

MOBILITY

The issue of mobility is discussed against the background of an increasingly mobile society generally; and church policies to minister more effectively, especially in the inner-city areas. Some of the free churches have traditionally had fairly mobile ministers, but readiness to be mobile seems to be increasingly expected across the board. At one time it would have been quite common for a minister to spend many years in one place, perhaps only ministering in two or three churches in his lifetime. It is now considered unusual to spend twenty, or even ten, years in one place.

There is a growing awareness that moving can be a costly business in human terms, and there is a great deal more we could do to soften the impact of mobility on ministers and their families. This is important in safeguarding their physical and mental health, and the quality of their ministry.

We should consider what losses are involved when a minister moves from one church to another. At the top of the list comes the home. It is well known that moving house is one of the more stressful experiences for anyone to go through, in terms of the effort and adjustment required. The welcoming church can help enormously by ensuring that practical details are taken care of *before* the minister arrives. One newly married couple moved to their first ministry to find that there was no telephone, and that the kitchen consisted of little more than a cold tap and a primus stove. The building and decorating work which carried on around them for the first few months greatly added to the stress of the many adjustments that they were making. Housing problems are common for ministers in many denominations, and do not reflect a loving, caring concern. The minister, especially a junior one, is often expected to accept standards which those making the decisions would not tolerate themselves.

Love and concern for the minister and his family can be expressed in so many practical ways, especially during times of transition; providing the basics is only a start. Bringing round a meal, a bunch of flowers, or helping to move the furniture, can be very welcoming and heart-warming.

Moving house may also be required during the course of a particular ministry. In the anglican church this may arise as part of the policy of changing from large old vicarages to smaller and newer housing. The Society of Mary and Martha has come across cases in several churches where the main reason for moving was financial expediency, even though alternative options were available. It is a big thing to expect a single person, still more a family, to move house on someone else's say-so, and church authorities would do well to take account of the additional stress they are imposing. By living in tied accommodation ministers forfeit a highly valued security in our home-owning society. This needs to be respected and not abused.

Another loss is the job itself, and with it the known routine and status within the community. There is a degree of familiarity, of feeling in control of the situation, which comes with having been in a job for a few years. Even if that particular ministry has been difficult, by moving on the minister will find himself a 'new boy' again, having to learn the ropes and earn acceptance.

Moving may well be a time of high expectations and excitement; indeed, it is important that it should be so. We come back to 'commitment, control and challenge' combining as 'hardiness' in the face of stressful events. A move which is seen as well timed, which leaves a job well done and looks forward to the challenge of the next stage in development, has a far more positive impact on health than one which is unwelcome or comes at a time when reserves of energy are low.

There are many more potential losses to be encountered during a move, which should not be underestimated. We understand so little about the whole area of cultural adjustments. Listening to migrants and refugees telling their stories reveals how much we are affected by our culture consciously and deeply within us. A move to another church is not as profound as a move to another

33

continent, but there may still be great differences in attitudes, in 'the way things are done here', in what is acceptable and what is not. Some of these are easily learned, but sometimes it can take many years to 'belong' to a community in any real sense, especially in rural communities. You may still be a newcomer after twenty years! Much of our individual security comes from 'belonging' in this sense. Our ultimate security as Christians comes from God, but he also created us as social beings with needs to relate to each other, to care for each other, to belong to each other. Without this we fail to be fully human. When faced with repeated needs to make fundamental adjustments, to transfer our 'belonging' from one group to another, the tendency is to withdraw into self-sufficiency as a less vulnerable option. On an individual level this may be a necessary self-protection, but it is a mistake to promote policies which reinforce it. People should not be automatically expected to move on simply because they have done a three- or five-year stint, the reasons need to be thought through rather more carefully.

Friendships and extended family ties are also jeopardised by mobility. It is important to take this into account and make the nurture of lifelong friendships a high priority. Ministers coming straight from the collegiality of their training into a strange church value continuing bonds of friendship which help to promote the feeling of belonging. This rootedness and security in one area can enable you to continue to give of yourself within the church when you might otherwise need to hold back for self-protection. Some people are more naturally able to put down roots in new situations than others, so again it is important to know yourself, to have some idea of how you are likely to respond, and hence know what your needs are during periods of transition.

Stability for members of the minister's family is also affected by moving. Traditionally, it is the wife who takes on much of the responsibility of making the new house into a home. Some churches are very warm in their welcome of the new family, but the wife who finds it difficult to get to know people will have less opportunity to do so than the minister for whom such meeting is part of the job. If the wife has a job then that will also be lost with the move. The wife will then be job-hunting without the freedom of mobility. The loss will be greater if they move to an area where there are no ready outlets for the wife's talents. Churches are increasingly having to adjust to the needs of double-ministry marriages, for whom mobility is a key problem.

For the children moving school is not just an issue during the examination years, when the academic side of things is interrupted. They, too, have the same needs as adults to belong and feel secure - at school, in the community, and in the home. Moving at any age takes adjustment. Their emotional support will generally need to be provided by the parents, which puts extra demands on them.

Too often, unfortunately, moves do not take place with the mentality of 'commitment, control and challenge'. With the loss of freehold it has become easier to move on anglican clergy who are seen as trouble-makers. But as we have seen, behavioural problems can be a symptom of stress. There are some ministers who are simply difficult, just as there are such people in every walk of life, but my impression is that they are not many. In many cases it can be argued that bad people-management has given rise to frustration and resentment, which should be tackled *in situ* rather than moving the problem elsewhere. Moderate, sensible people can become 'trouble-makers' when repeatedly faced with unreasonable situations and demands. In some free churches, the system of short-term ministries needing to be renewed by a large majority of the church before they can be extended is very open to abuse by uncaring members. There are sad stories of ministers being forced to move at a time when they were just beginning to feel that things were being achieved within the church, amid family difficulties regarding health and the children's education, etc. If the church as a whole cares for its ministers, such things need to be taken into account when moves are planned.

It is too easy to forget or ignore the fact that many, even most, of the unresolved problems move with one. For instance, a minister may be moved because he is under stress from the pressures of work. At first sight offering a move might seem to be a caring proposition, but sometimes the relevant questions have not been asked: Is the job simply too much for one person, anyway? If so, presumably the next person in the job will be similarly overloaded. It will eventually be necessary to restructure the job whether or not the minister moves. If the job is not too much for one person, why is this particular minister failing to cope? Does he have enough support? Does he need help in learning how to pace himself and evaluate his work? Are there other things, such as marriage difficulties, which contribute to the stress? Is he exhausted? A move alone will *solve* none of these problems. It will merely add to an already stressful situation.

It is more caring, and in the long run more economic, to try and deal with the real problems. Sometimes the underlying problems are well known to the superiors, but they have inadequate ideas or resources to resolve them. There are now many caring agencies such as the Society of Mary and Martha which are able to help, and they should be used. However, the burden of payment should not fall on the individual. With low salaries, the cost of professional help may discourage the minister from seeking help; churches need to have funds available for this purpose.

Exhaustion is particularly important in this context. People who are exhausted need rest. If a move is going ahead anyway, the church needs to provide accommodation and salary during the interim, sometimes for several months. If a move is decided against, a long break may still be needed, but it may be counter-productive to take this at home unless the congregation are very protective and disciplined against the use of the telephone and the door bell. Joan, the minister's wife of chapter one (p.2), was simply too exhausted to see any of the well-meaning members of the congregation who kept trying to visit her with 'good advice'. The effort of being nice to people was overwhelming, and only made her feel more guilty. The most effective and valued support she received was from someone who came in and cooked a meal each day, and looked after other practical matters in the house.

William had been under hospital investigation for several weeks before it was recognised that the stress of severe overwork was the major cause of his illness. He was given a generous bursary from area church funds to enable him and his wife to take a much needed two-week break in a hotel.

An acclimatisation period can be useful for any minister moving to a new church. In some places, curates are encouraged to spend at least the first month simply getting the feel of the neighbourhood, getting to know its people, and enabling their families to settle down. What a marked contrast this is to the vicar who found that the church council had delayed even the most trivial decisions for the entire nine months of the interregnum, and presented him with the whole backlog within the first few days of his arrival!

In summary, therefore, the mobility of ministers is a very valuable resource for the church. But the human and financial costs of abusing that resource are high. Superiors, colleagues, congregations and friends, can help the minister and his family make their move a positive experience; a little practical love can go a long way. Handled badly, the many potential areas of loss entailed in moving can be a threat to physical and mental health. If you are a minister faced with such a situation, it is important to *seek* help from friends, family, or caring agencies. Check the balance on your effort-and-distress axes. If the effort and distress cannot be reduced, find ways of increasing the relaxation and wellbeing.

7

KNOWING YOURSELF

The theme of knowing yourself underpins much of the approach to stress-management. But how do we know ourselves? Is it even desirable to take notice of our moods, feelings and emotions when such are so notoriously fickle? Does it mean seeing an analyst every five minutes? The most important thing is that each one of us is a unique child of God, created by him, and precious for who we are. There is a variety of schemes which divide people into 'personality types', but while these have their uses they are no substitute for a basic awareness of our inner selves - knowing who we are and what makes us tick.

Ministers are particularly vulnerable to the pressure of maintaining a 'good Christian' image, which generally means never being angry, aggressive, afraid, insecure, depressed, anxious or erotic. The question is: what happens to these feelings if they are experienced but not acknowledged or expressed? Many people try to live as though they are safely dead and buried. Often they are indeed buried, but they are buried alive, leaving us vulnerable to their effects in indirect ways. That is like burying nuclear waste, in the vain hope that we shall find a solution before the problems catch up with us.

This process of repression is often responsible for the apparent inconsistencies in our experience and behaviour, such as flying off the handle over a trivial incident which did not justify such a strong response; or getting terribly upset over a particular death and not understanding why; or seeing yourself becoming irritable with someone you love, and hating yourself for it. Was the anger really due to a succession of other incidents in which you were not allowed to be angry, or related to an incident in your childhood? Was the unexpected grief reaction really to do with a previous ungrieved loss of a person, or an ideal? Was the irritation

38

really against yourself, though expressed in a destructive way to those closest to you?

Expressing emotions
Dealing well with feelings is not only important to our mental health and stability. We saw in chapter two how closely emotional experiences are linked with physical changes. Those changes, which are potentially damaging to the body, take place with the experience of emotions, whether or not there is any outward expression of them. That is not to say that we should be aiming for a bland, unemotional existence to protect our health, but rather that we need to learn how to release and express emotions in a constructive way; how to stop negative emotions festering away and causing damage underneath the surface.

The situation which provokes feelings is often not the appropriate place to express them. If someone makes you angry it is not generally conducive to good relationships to punch him on the nose, although it might make you feel better! What you can do is release the tension later with a brisk walk, or have a good yell where no one will hear you, or beat the daylights out of an old cushion. There will be situations which upset you, but where it is more appropriate to have a good cry later. Equally, there are many occasions when we bottle-up our feelings through embarrassment or anxiety, when it would be quite appropriate to express them.

Even when feelings are nasty, destructive or 'unchristian', it is still important to acknowledge them and accept God's love for us, warts an' all. The way forward is to invite God in to heal and change us from within. Maturity in Christ involves an ongoing change of heart in a very deep sense, whereby those feelings gradually disappear. This is different from having the feelings but not expressing them. We each need to find our own ways of working things through, and learn to bring the debris to God for healing. For some it will be right to explore things in some depth with a psychoanalyst; others will want to talk things through with a friend, a counsellor or a spiritual director; and some may benefit from a sensitive ministry of inner healing for past hurts. We should expect to need the help of other people along our journey.

Guilt is another big headache. Jesus came to set us free from guilt, but as Christians we are very good at piling it back very quickly. There are important distinctions between spiritual guilt, which comes from sinning in God's eyes, and psychological guilt which comes from not living up to the expectations of yourself or other people. The first needs repentance before God; but the second can actually be made worse by treating it as a spiritual malady. When the guilt feelings do not go away, the guilt of spiritual failure adds to the misery. This emotional/human guilt can be dealt with by talking things through with someone else, especially if this enables you to take a fresh perspective on things. It is surprising how much relief people gain by simply getting things off their chest.

Personal growth

I like the poster, 'Be patient with me - God has not finished with me yet'. We may know in theory that living as a Christian is a process of growth, a journey not a destination; but ministers get manoeuvred into pretending that they have already arrived. You are expected to be a model of perfection, rather than a fellow-pilgrim. A good deal of tension is caused by teaching what you believe to be right, while at the same time being aware of not meeting that standard yourself. People are only too quick to point out when you fail to practise what you preach, which is a very vulnerable position to be in.

Being vulnerable is painful. We do not like to be faced with vulnerability, either in ourselves or in others. We feel uncomfortable, and require the reassurance that everything is okay. But at the same time there is something essentially strong and Christ-like about allowing other people to see our struggles, disappointments and failures. Facing and dealing with our own darkness will enable others to grow, too.

Loving people

Hugh Eadie[1] developed the concept of the 'helping personality', after interviews with about one hundred Scottish clergymen in the early 1970s. This is the personality of someone whose principal motivation is to be helpful and concerned with other people. They tend to choose the 'helping professions', such as social work, nursing or medicine, or enter the Christian ministry. Such people will tend to have a natural warmth and love for people, but they are also entering a ministry where loving others is an unwritten part of the job description. It is very easy for confusion to arise over the different motivations for loving:

1. Desire to love - I freely choose to love you
2. Need to love - loving you fulfils my need to love
3. Obligation to love - I love you because I ought to.

The first is the generous, unconditional love which God has for us, in which he invites us to share. In our relationships with others, it is the Christ-like love which asks for nothing in return. You can end up feeling very guilty when it is a struggle to love freely, but God does not require us to have arrived - only to be moving in the right direction.

The need to love is present to some extent in all of us. It helps to fulfil our need to be thought of as warm, caring people, and often brings the reward of being loved in return. It is good to receive and appreciate love when it is returned, but if this becomes a major motivation for caring, then the therapeutic relationship turns into a parasitic one. Instead of allowing people to be free, there can be subtle manoeuvring to make people dependent on us. It can become like the parent-child relationship of 'How could you do this to me, after all I've done for you?' Adult relationships need to be about mutual love and dependence, rather than based on guilt.

The obligation to love can easily become a trap. We are commanded to love our neighbour as ourselves. This is often translated to mean that we must always be meek and mild, have loving feelings and be generally lovable people. This is invariably attempted in our own strength and, indeed, at the expense of our real selves. The caring concern is a very real part of the personality and is not being faked, but problems can arise because other aspects have to be supressed in the interests of maintaining the loving image. This obligation is both self-imposed and reinforced by people who expect the minister to live up to this standard all day, every day. Failure is almost guaranteed and brings yet more guilt.

People often think they should try to love harder if the feelings are not there. Effort may indeed be needed for growth on the up-slope of the human function curve; but for someone who is exhausted and on the downslope, further effort is part of the self-destruct mode. Just being with people can become enormously draining.

Brian, a 45-year old minister, went through a period of exhaustion in which he barely managed to take services and the very thought of socialising afterwards made him feel exhausted. He felt very guilty about his apparent lack of love for his congregation, and things got considerably worse. Fortunately he had a very sensible doctor who recognised the problem and signed him off for two months' sick-leave, with instructions not to see anyone. The five years since that time have been the most productive yet in his ministry. His problem was a physical one, although it appeared to be spiritual.

In an attempt to prove himself loving by human efforts, the minister may have to resort to working excessive hours, being on call twenty-four hours a day, seven days a week, as well as being a model of dedication and commitment. It may indeed be part of the minister's calling to be a very available and caring person, but if God had intended us to be gods, he would not have made us human. When the image of helper grows out of proportion, it becomes very difficult to allow ourselves opportunities for rest and relaxation, or to seek help when we need it. In the effort to love everyone, we end up building great defences against being loved ourselves.

Working hard - for what?
It is interesting to compare Eadie's idea of 'the helping personality' with the clinical observations of Freudenberger, an American psychoanalyst, and one of the first to develop the concept of burnout. He describes some of the characteristics of people vulnerable to burnout:[2]

1. Need to be liked and accepted, therefore find it hard to say no
2. Sensitive to disappointment and loneliness
3. Often loners in childhood

4. Selfless to the point of being drained
5. Need to experience most of their gratification in life
   through their work (rather than family or hobbies, etc)

He concludes that

the therapist needs to assist the client to reflect on, clarify, and eventually change personal values, dedication, commitment, caring too much ... that have helped to promote burnout ... helping the person to prioritize and evaluate these values, which values are his own, which have been imposed by family, and which are a function of the organisation and society.

One is tempted to add 'which have been imposed by the therapist?' This widely quoted concept that stress and burnout are a direct consequence of dedication, commitment and caring too much, leads many ministers to feel that there is a straight choice between taking care of themselves, or doing the work to which they are called. Most ministers want to be dedicated, committed and caring, and would rather burn out than have to change that. Fortunately, the two can be combined. The key question is whether these values spring from the heart, from God's love at work within us, or whether they are the outworkings of our own anxiety and guilt or a desperate attempt to prove ourselves and be loved.

Sometimes it is not hard to see from where internalised pressures originate. Ron is a priest nearing retirement, whose only holidays in a lifelong ministry have been during prolonged convalescence after illness. As a boy his father was continually pushing him to achieve; to do 'great things for God'; never to waste a minute in the day, for 'the devil finds work for idle hands'. Throughout his life his father has expressed disapproval of days off, of holidays, of anything other than hard work. Anyone subjected to this kind of pressure begins to internalise at least some of it. The periods of convalescence were the only times he was able to justify not working to himself, or to his father. The illnesses were not feigned or engineered, but were a very necessary internal defence mechanism against the punishing expectations under which he lived.

Studies of Roman catholic nuns,[3] and other religious communities, have shown that long hours and hard work can be sustained very well while people feel there is purpose and meaning in their work. Loss of commitment is found to be a major precursor of burnout. This contrasts with the idea that it is simply those who work too hard who burn out. Effort combined with the distress of meaningless and loss of ideals is what is dangerous.

Being and doing

Another issue of particular relevance to ministers is the mixing of work and personal identity. To some extent the two cannot be separated - ministry requires that you give of yourself, and the ministry you offer is intimately related to who you are as a person. But each of us has a 'being' self which is essentially valuable to God in its own right. Our value as people does not depend on our 'doing'. A minister who comes in for a lot of criticism and finds it hard to see much in the way of positive results, will all too easily end up feeling a worthless failure.

It has been observed that ministers as a group tend to have a low self-esteem. This is not good for health, and more importantly is a failure to see ourselves as God sees us - as infinitely precious children. We preach a gospel of justification by faith, but tend to feel and act as if our own justification depends on works. I do not suppose that any of us have even begun to comprehend the depth and tenderness of God's love for us. Sometimes we need to learn to relax and accept that love rather than strive to be worthy of it.

8

HOME LIFE, MARRIAGE AND FAMILY

It is often said that most churches want their minister to be a married bachelor. Married, to prove that he is normal (i.e. not homosexual), to have a built-in answer-phone service, and because 'family men are better able to relate to those with family problems'. And single to have endless time and energy for helping others without being tied down by the demands of domestic pressures. The two covenants of marriage and ministry can enhance each other or come into bitter conflict.

Much of this chapter addresses the situation of married male ministers, but with the growing number of female ministers - married either to other ministers or to men in different jobs - I imagine that much applies to their situations as well.

In a recent Australian survey quoted by Robin Pryor,[1] 57% of ministers responding indicated that their spouse was their 'most important source of support and encouragement'. A stable, loving relationship is an invaluable resource for coping with stress. But marital problems or failure among ministers cause even more distress than usual, due to the glare of publicity and the expectation that a minister should set a good example in such things. Couples who get into difficulty feel extremely guilty, and very isolated with problems which are actually quite common. Although people are always horrified when ministers' marriages go wrong, there is a remarkably low priority placed on enrichment and growth between couples in the ministry. Love needs nurturing, just as much as faith. This chapter examines some of the major stresses and pitfalls in order to enable couples to share problems more constructively with each other, and with others if necessary.

Housing

There is no doubt that marriages in the ministry come under pressures which are not normally experienced by those outside it. Firstly, there is the intrusion of privacy which comes from the minister working from home. Although some churches now have offices where the minister does a more 'normal' working day, the majority still work from home. This means that people will be telephoning or calling at all times of the day - and night. Meal times are often the only time when the couple try to snatch half an hour together, but people call then, 'because I knew I'd catch you in'. If the minister is out, people will often expect the spouse or even the children to provide information, take messages, or offer a listening ear. Some ministers find it useful to make known specific 'family times', and ask church members to avoid calling then.

If the minister's house is used as an office and for meetings, there will be a considerable amount of traffic through the house. In addition to the interruptions and wear and tear on the furnishings, it means that intimate details of family life are exposed to public view in a way to which 'normal' families are not accustomed. Some people will feel very free to comment on the unwashed laundry, the piles of washing up, or the undusted furniture; not to mention one's methods of child care, choice of toys or bed-times. Such thoughtless comments can be very distressing even for the most competent wife and mother, especially if combined with such comments as, '. . . and I would have thought you should be setting a good example.' Being welcomed into another person's home is an enormous privilege, no less so because the church happens to own the bricks and mortar.

The question of housing is often a troubled one. Churches often expect the minister and his family to make do with standards of repair, heating, plumbing, wiring and decoration which members would not accept in their own homes. It is humiliating to have to ask repeatedly for basic repairs to be done, but the Society of Mary and Martha has come across many situations where this has been a major and ongoing stress for individuals and families in ministry.

Traditional vicarages and manses are often large and hard to keep heated and furnished. However, they do give the family privacy and space even though the house is being heavily used. The newer, smaller vicarages may be more suitable in some ways, but families who wish to run an open house as part of their ministry can end up being very short-changed. There is a danger of insisting on a bureaucratic uniformity in housing without taking into account the very different needs of families.

There is also the problem of retirement accommodation. Provision does seem to be improving in some churches, but most ministry couples will be having to think about uprooting and house-hunting at a time when other people can relax and enjoy the fruits of their labours. There is no easy answer though, as many would be reluctant to stay on 'under the feet' of the new minister in any case. Ministers are often told they have an easy existence because they are provided with a house and have no mortgage bills to pay. They pay the price when they retire, and their children forfeit property inheritance later.

Time off

Without the sensitivity and co-operation of members of the church and local community, it can be very difficult for ministers to take time off at home. Many people do not understand or respect the need that couples have simply to spend time together; they do not take kindly to being asked to come back another day if the minister is not visibly 'doing' something. It takes nerves of steel to let the telephone ring, without worrying if it might be family, or something vitally important. Some find answer-phones a useful aid, but others dislike their impersonal nature. Some churches have a system whereby calls are diverted to another colleague or member of the church on the minister's day off. This would seem to be the best of all worlds, but requires a committed and responsible team.

There are different ideas of what 'taking time off' actually means. For some, priority is given for six full days a week to strictly church-related work or ministry. Shopping, decorating, gardening, cleaning the car, reading etc., are all relegated to the day off. It is no surprise when it ends up just as frantic as the other six days of the week. But who wants to 'get caught' in the supermarket when they are supposed to be at work?

The Jewish sabbath was a day of rest, but not just rest from paid work. It also entails a memorial of the exodus from Egypt, stressing both servitude to God and freedom from servitude to human masters. Often it is we ourselves who are our own cruel taskmasters. The sabbath is God's special gift of freedom from 'I must' and 'I ought'.

Jim, a married minister in his fifties, lived with a frantic 'day off' for many years, until forced to take three months off work from exhaustion. He is now cheerfully back, and has chosen a more balanced way of life. Each week he takes a full day to read, study and meditate, to allow 'input' for himself and his sermons and teaching. His day off is usually spent with his wife and their children, and he has no qualms about shopping or doing odd jobs about the house on 'work' days. A few years ago he did not believe it was possible to work like this and still fit everything in. It is interesting to hear that he now feels his ministry is more positive and productive than before. But a word of warning: these changes can be suggested and encouraged by colleagues and family, but they will only be effective if they come from a change of attitude in oneself. However well-meaning, enforced relaxation is a very stressful experience because it entails guilt and frustration. Church members can help enormously by showing that they regard marriage and family time as important. When the couple are out shopping or going for a walk, a comment like, 'Nice to see you enjoying yourselves together' is more helpful than, 'So this is what you get up to when our backs are turned!'.

Children

Ministers are often busy in the evenings and at weekends. This means that if the spouse has a job with normal working week hours or the children are at school, it can be even more difficult to structure time off together. There are potentially a lot of perks in growing up as a minister's child, but children are very vulnerable to the pressures of a 'goldfish bowl' existence, especially as it is not of their choosing. Parents may need to fight very hard to protect them from expectations of conformity. Teenagers go through 'difficult' periods, often to do with establishing their identity and place in the world. They, too, need space to be themselves, and not to have to live up to the expectations of their peers, church members or parents. It is to be expected that they will need an adult confidant outside the family even though (or because?) their father is the minister. Children get hurt when it seems that everyone else has a call on their parents' time and there is none left for them.

Support for families

Family relationships, like any others, suffer when they are neglected. Family loyalties, and the scandal of 'trouble at the vicarage' mean that seeking help with relationships is often delayed too long. But to whom can the family turn when they want to seek help? To go to anyone who knows the minister as a colleague or a superior could bring further embarrassment, as could confiding in a member of the church. The wider family can be a great support, but its members may be living at a distance and relatives cannot always offer objective advice.

It is clear that the various confidential counselling and support services which are springing up around the country are vitally important. The individual, couple or family can get help outside their local area and denominational or church structures. This is a great encouragement to seeking early help without fear of gossip. Marriage breakdown among ministry couples was formerly one of the unthinkable events, both for the couple and the wider church. The couple often has to live out vicariously other people's fantasy of the ideal marriage; with the bonus of help from the Almighty they simply should not get into trouble! And yet Broken Rites now estimate that within the anglican church alone there is at least one marriage breakdown per diocese each year. Ministry marriages are not immune to failure, and with the extra pressures preventative work is especially important.

Hilary Devereux[2] interviewed a selection of anglican clergy deserted by their wives. Many blamed their own over-involvement in parish affairs for their failure to realise how unhappy their wives were until the relationship was irrevocably damaged.

49

Richard and Sue had a busy social life, and enjoyed gardening together until Richard entered the ministry in his late forties. Facing great cultural and financial changes, Sue felt in need of Richard's support but was dismayed when he threw himself into church work with such enjoyment that he seldom spent time with her. Richard found that after meeting people's needs all day, he wanted Sue to show him love and affection when he came home, not demand it from him. She became angry and bitter, and threatened to leave on several occasions. It was a chance conversation with a friend which made Richard realise that Sue was getting a raw deal, but it seemed that whatever he offered, she was never satisfied. Fortunately they sought professional help before it was too late, and agreed areas of mutual compromise. Making small changes helped to provide foundations on which they were able to rebuild a happy marriage.

It is all too easy to take those close to us for granted, especially when we are busy or tired. That is why it is so important to make 'quality time' for each other, and not just make do with the dregs once everything else has had its share. This applies to the physical side of marriage, as well as the other areas. If the minister is regularly coming home tired from late meetings the couple's sex life will often deteriorate. Make time to make love in the afternoon!

Ministers' wives

We have not yet tackled the touchy subject of whether or not ministers'wives should take a job outside the home. Many feel they need to do so out of sheer economic necessity. Stipends may be generous compared with what some people in our supposedly affluent society have to live on, but they are very low in relation to the social status of ministers. This can be especially hard in middle-class churches where there is a subtle censure of failure to live up to the expected standards of dress and entertaining. Families do have different needs and expectations. Some are quite able to manage on meagre resources, and others genuinely have a great struggle to make ends meet. In a society of plastic money, ministry families are also at risk of taking the credit card route into debt.

Sensitive advice and help is needed in this area, but preferably not 'charity' handouts.

Wives also take jobs for other reasons. The stereotype of a minister's wife is just as pervasive as that of her husband. Some women are very fulfilled in their traditional role, and contribute much to their husband's ministry. Others could find it rewarding but are terrified by the expectation that they will step into the shoes of the last super-capable 'Mrs Minister' rather than develop their own unique ministry. Others may be very unhappy in this role, or may be called to other work in their own right. Ministry couples are having to work out their own solutions against a background of rapid change in the expectations of both male and female roles. The tensions regarding their individual careers and needs, whose take priority and so on, are magnified when one or both are considered to be doing 'God's work'. The solutions are as varied as the people in the situations, and the most valuable thing a couple can be offered is loving support as they seek the right answers for them as a couple.

9

STRESS AND SPIRITUALITY

Spiritual growth and development is central to stress-management, but it is vital to begin from the right point. The central purpose of our lives is to come to love God more fully, and allow ourselves to be more fully loved by him; everything springs from this. To see spiritual growth as a means to its own ends (even if those ends are as worthy as equipping ourselves for his service) is to lose the very God we seek. The danger is that prayer can become just another form of 'self-improvement' - or even a 'stress management technique'.

Having said that, there is no doubt that the maturing of our relationship with God brings a truer perspective and meaning which is vital in learning to live with and through the stress, rather than trying to avoid it, or being crushed by it. Spirituality does not bring immunity from stress, and it is sad and damaging that ministers suffering from stress are often seen as spiritual failures. 'Pray harder' is just the pseudo-spiritual version of 'try harder' which is so damaging to exhausted people.

The important thing is that we take our spiritual growth seriously on a regular basis rather than wait for times of crisis. Surrounded by a hundred and one needs, it is understandable that study and prayer so often get squeezed out, but when this happens the minister is in danger of losing the uniqueness of his ministry, of becoming a do-gooder with a dog-collar. A basic question is whether the minister is primarily called to serve God, or to serve the people of God? The call to serve people can easily mean that the priority becomes the meeting of *their* needs and expectations, which leads to exhaustion, resentment, guilt and failure. When the call is understood to serve God, the priority falls on becoming a redeemed and compassionate person, suffering *with* people not *because* of them.

Darkness and doubt

A major obstacle to growth is the fact that ministers are expected to be spiritual 'experts' and not subject to doubts or difficulties like ordinary mortals. Many ministers feel that they are spiritual failures, and struggle on alone for years feeling guilty for failing God and anxious about being exposed as frauds. The minister has far more at stake with his faith than most members of his church. If he loses his faith, he is faced with the choice of losing his credibility, his job and his home, or being a hypocrite by teaching what he does not believe. When normal, healthy doubting and questioning carry these undertones of fear and anxiety, they become major stresses in their own right, and fear is a very potent block to that openness which is needed for growth.

It is all too easy to talk glibly about the 'dark nights of the soul' when dealing with the distressing experiences of not knowing where God is, of not knowing even whether he exists. But growth often occurs in periods of transition and then consolidation, rather than in a smooth process. During those transitions, things which before seemed very certain and dependable may suddenly be lost. We all like to feel in control, and part of that control is the feeling that we understand what is going on, and know it is safe. But God has a habit of pulling the rug of security out from under our feet in the process of teaching us to be more dependent on him. The frightening part is when we lose a whole way of understanding and relating to God. What feels like a loss of faith is really the loss of an inadequate image of God. In time he will reveal himself in new and deeper ways, but the period of transition is often one of confusion and uncertainty.

Faith development

Jim Fowler[1] has attempted to chart a path of faith-development, in much the same way as others have charted intellectual and psychological development. His stages do not relate to the *content* of faith, but to the *way* in which you believe. Thus there is a progression from simple acceptance of whatever you were taught as a child; going on to choose what to accept and what to reject during adolescence; followed by stages of certainties; being able to hold opposites in tension; and, finally, moving on to the deceptively simple faith of full maturity. Many of us get stuck at this or that stage along the way, either because we are comfortable where we are or because the unknown is too frightening. Ministers know adults who have never matured from the child's understanding of God, whose faith falls apart when faced with major crisis. Such people have the choice of rejecting God completely because he appears to have failed them, or of moving to a deeper faith; transition from an adult faith to a more mature one can be just as frightening and painful.

The development of inner spiritual resources is important for all Christians, but especially for ministers who are in the front line in dealing with the suffering and questioning of others. A growing faith is vital in order to continue to meet their deep needs with compassion and hope. Spiritual antennae need to be developed, which bring a sensitivity to people and the true nature of their needs - not just from expertise in counselling skills. But spiritual maturity brings with it more stress. As we come closer to the heart of God there is a growing identification with the suffering of people, and we are drawn into the godly struggle for justice and peace. A mature Christian by definition cannot be wholly comfortable in a society such as ours.

Finding stillness with God is important if we are to allow the muddy waters of busyness to settle, and permit our seeing with clarity and vision. We need to discern between the creative struggles which come from living out God's compassion for a broken world and the unnecessary, draining struggles of our own or others' making. Stillness and silence provide important pathways both to the knowledge of ourselves and of God, as well as being valuable training in listening pastorally to others. But the stillness is not some sort of spiritual tranquilliser to help us feel peaceful, though this is a welcome gift when it comes. Rather, it is part of the unsettling and challenging process of learning to embody the peace of God.

One of the areas of stress-management which is often omitted in 'secular' thinking, is that of 'meaning' in life. Stress is so often associated with activity and too much work that we ignore the deeper problems associated with meaninglessness. It was revealing to see a television interviewer enquiring how the life of aborigines on welfare benefit in shanty towns could be described as stressful, when 'all they had to do was sit under a tree all day'! As Christians we are greatly privileged to have meaning in life at the most fundamental level. It is one of the most valuable resources we have in managing stress. But because it is so important, it leaves ministers who are going through periods of major doubt in either their faith or their vocation especially vulnerable to stress. They desperately need people with whom they can share their doubts and struggles without fear of rejection or censure if they are successfully to work through such periods. According to American and Australian research quoted by Robin Pryor,[2] there are very few ministers indeed who leave their ministry because of a comprehensive loss of faith. Usually it is either because of a *change* in their personal faith, because of disillusionment with church structures, or because of personal or family inability to cope with the pressures.

Having a spiritual director is very valuable in keeping up the impetus of positive growth rather than only thinking about it when problems arise. Gordon Jeff[3] provides a very down-to-earth approach to the subject, dispelling the myth that spiritual direction is only for the elite 'hot house blooms of the soul'. You would meet with a director two or three times a year to discus progress and problems on your spiritual journey. The spiritual director is someone who is able to give guidance, and who is far enough removed from the daily shopping-list of ups and downs to discern trends more clearly. He is there to provide signposts along the way rather than props; the true Director, of course, is the Holy Spirit.

Retreats

Carving out a time each day to be quiet with God is very important, as are regular periods of retreat. While holidays and further training are important, it is of concern that they are often given a higher priority than times of quiet for spiritual refreshment. At home there are always so many distractions, interruptions; things which need to be done urgently. There is no substitute for going away for a period, whether a day, a week or more. There are many organised retreats available, and religious houses are often very pleased to give people a few days away from it all. The declining numbers of such houses means that the churches should be considering very carefully where ministers may go for times of quiet. Both the older and the newer houses need much better support from the churches as they are a vital resource.

One of the problems with retreats is that many people who are hurt or under stress are not emotionally in a position to make use of concentrated silence. An emotional problem may have been misdiagnosed as a spiritual one. You may have experienced going away for a time of quiet only to find yourself ministering to other retreatants whose clamourous needs prevented you from dealing with your own. This was one of the factors which led to the development of the Society of Mary and Martha's '12,000-mile service' weeks. By having a high ratio of 'helpers', we are able to offer people a lot of human warmth and attention. Guests are specifically requested not to try and minister to each other's needs so that each person is enabled to deal with his own agenda. People who are accustomed to being in helping roles find it very difficult not to respond when faced with other people's need, but they too need times of quiet and refreshment. When planning a retreat, try and identify what it is that you need: is it complete quiet for time with God? A guided retreat? Or an opportunity to explore new aspects of your spirituality within a group? Do you need physical rest, or a chance to talk things through with someone before you can use a formal retreat effectively?

Meditation

There are so many different approaches to prayer, and so many books about prayer that it can be difficult to know where to start. A good spiritual director is likely to be able to suggest what might suit you as an individual, help iron out the difficulties and dispel any guilt which arises because of the failure of one particular method. I include here something on meditation, not because it is necessarily the best way to pray, but because it is particularly relevant to spirituality in the context of stress and stress-management.

Many people were frightened from meditation in the sixties, because of its associations with oriental culture and spirituality. We are now more aware of the long Christian tradition of meditation, and its value in spiritual growth. Some people are natural contemplatives, but for others it comes less easily. For those learning from scratch it is a good idea to start with simple relaxation exercises and body-awareness, not because this is meditation in the strictly spiritual sense but because physical stillness and relaxation is an important prelude to mental and spiritual stillness. If you carry a lot of mental clutter and worry, the whole time can be used just for relaxing in God's presence and being cherished by Him. External quiet and physical stillness help to cut down on the distractions, especially in the early stages. Chapter 13 (pp. 77) provides some help in getting started with relaxation if you are not already familiar with these techniques.

The next step is to choose a word, a phrase or an image from scripture or other helpful source, or a picture on which to dwell. If other thoughts intrude, gently return to your chosen theme when you become aware that you have wandered. Allow your chosen theme to become part of you, to reach not just your mind or intellect but to sink into your heart and soul. It is here, deep down, that we can be exposed to the changing, healing power of God; where we can meet with the God of peace rather than simply seeking the peace of God. Sometimes meditation appears to bring nothing but great emptiness and dryness, while at other times there is an intense awareness of being loved by God in a way which draws us to respond in praise and thanksgiving. All we need to do is to offer ourselves to God, and be open to him rather than seek good experiences. When we offer ourselves in this way, changes happen within us whether we are immediately aware of them or not.

10

SPECIAL NEEDS

We have already discussed the stressfulness of a minister's life, and some of the consequences of being under too much stress. This chapter highlights some of the people who are at higher risk because of extra stresses. Keep an eye open for those for whom you are pastorally responsible in any of these groups, as well as colleagues or even superiors. You may be able to offer them much needed support, or mobilise extra resources in their direction. If you come into any of these groups yourself, be aware of the extra needs you may have and add them into your distress and effort equation.

Women in ministry
There is a growing number of women in full-time ministry. They often find that they have to fulfil not only their role as a minister, but also that of a minister's wife. For example, a female minister is more likely to be expected to produce cakes for a coffee morning or join in cleaning or flower rotas than her male colleagues. Many are faced with subtle but damaging stress from male colleagues who may disagree with women being in the ministry at all. While everyone has a right to his own views, it is wrong to put extra stress deliberately onto people who are trying to minister to others. As in many other male-dominated professions, women tend to feel that they have to prove themselves by working even harder than their male colleagues. As these colleagues are probably overworking themselves, this is hardly a recipe for stress reduction!

Married women ministers endeavour to run a home and a family in addition to their work, and tend to feel guilty and stressed from not doing either as well as they would want to. This is not the place to argue the rights or wrongs of working wives and mothers. The point is that when they do, they will be under more stress than a less involved person - male or female - doing the same job, and therefore need more by way of support.

Double career marriages are now commonplace in society as a whole, but the church has not yet come to grips with the changing needs of such couples. If both are in the ministry, family time and holidays become even harder to maintain. It also has a major influence on their mobility, and church authorities are often not good at taking family needs into account, let alone the career needs of a spouse. It can be very frustrating for a minister to move for the sake of their spouse's job, only to find themselves not needed as a minister in their new locality.

Ministers' wives

The Society of Mary and Martha was set up with the needs of active ministers very much in mind. But it has rapidly become clear how much need there is among ministers' wives, divorced wives, widows, and people who have left the ministry for one reason or another - people who are intimately involved with the church, but who largely fall outside the orbit of pastoral care of the hierarchy or denominational headquarters.

Ministers' wives are as much in the front line as the minister, especially when he works from home. She will often be the one who answers the telephone, the door, takes messages, and deals with people when he is out. But ministers' wives are no more of a homogeneous group than the ministers themselves. Some will want to be actively involved in their partner's ministry, and equally supported by the church authorities. Others do not, and feel affronted by any direct overtures in this direction. Within the anglican church, care of the clergy's wives often falls to the wife of the archdeacon or the bishop. While they may be very good in this role, they are no more automatically equipped to do so than the average minister's wife is equipped to perform the parish duties expected of her. Moreover, ministers are often very concerned about 'black marks' going in the book if they take problems to their superiors; and their wives are frequently even more concerned about this. Their problems are often tied up with work and relationships within the home, not least the stresses under which they see their husbands. The question, as they see it, is one of disloyalty, and so they feel that there is no one to whom they can turn. Independent care of families is greatly needed.

Death and divorce

A clergy widow or divorcee is faced with massive losses just at a time when she can least be expected to cope with them. In quick succession she loses her husband, her status, her social role and her home. The stresses of loss were discussed in chapter six (p. 32ff.) but it is not realised how acutely they apply in these situations. All these losses are faced at a time when she is trying to cope with her own, at times, overwhelming emotions, and care for bewildered children as well. Diane was actually left completely homeless for two months, and that only eight months after her husband had died, due to delays and incompetence on the part of those responsible for re-housing her. She was forced to put her belongings into store and stay with various friends until her new home was ready. How uncaring! Widows often feel that they ought to move out of the locality to avoid being an embarrassment to the next incumbent, so they also lose the very people who might have been most able to support them in re-building their lives.

Broken Rites have campaigned vigorously on behalf of divorced or separated wives over the last few years, so in the anglican church there are at least formal structures for practical care to ensure that separated wives and their families do not fall through the net completely. How well the system actually works varies according to the people involved, and the priority placed on this ministry. In any marriage break-up there are enormous feelings of guilt and blame for both parties. These are greatly increased in the situation where the couple are in the public eye, where gossip and censure are rife. A good deal of thought and sensitivity is needed in order to ensure that all parties receive adequate care and support.

The problems of widowed or divorced ministers are just as acute, although their needs are different. A bereaved minister will need a lot of practical and emotional support for at least a year in order to do his job and work through what is often very public grief.

A minister whose marriage breaks up may or may not forfeit his job and house. Whether he leaves the ministry or stays in it, he will need as much care and help to re-build his life as his former wife will.

Leaving the ministry
Some of the more common reasons for leaving the ministry[1] include:

> disillusion with the relevance of the church to the
>   modern world
> failure to enjoy the work
> inadequate stipend and/or accommodation
> spouse and/or family unhappy
> feeling inadequate or unrespected as a church leader
> uncertain of vocation
> change in personal faith
> the offer of more attractive work or training opportunities

People also find themselves out of ministry as a result of ill-health, marriage break-down or misbehaviour. The feelings of rejection and alienation are great. They continue to have spiritual and emotional needs, but they are people whose needs the church finds it very hard to meet. When Stuart resigned from his parish after the break-up of his marriage, he found that he and his new partner Jacky were not able to receive Holy Communion together in any of the local churches. They were effectively ostracised, just at a time when they most needed support.

Ministers who have left because of ill-health or family needs tend to engender feelings of embarrassment and discomfort if they seek to remain as members of a congregation. Above all, they will feel like failures, and may be seen as such: we do not want to be confronted by people who are living reminders of our own potential problems or failures. Anyone leaving the ministry, especially if he is leaving in disgrace, is in need of pastoral care. If his superior has had to enforce discipline, he may not be able to offer that care himself, but he needs to ensure that someone is doing so.

Unmarried ministers

Single people tend to have a greater need for friendships, for people with whom they can share both the problems and the good things in life. Without someone to help put a right perspective on things, it can be easy to get despondent when things appear to go badly. Some people are called to marriage and others to the single life, but none of us is called to live in isolation. Human warmth and friendship are important, and single people can find themselves incredibly lonely without it. The trouble with being lonely is that you can seem to swallow people whole when they do appear! So the pressure puts them off, increasing the vicious circle of loneliness. Take a good look at the aspects of support discussed in the next chapter, and see if you can find people to meet specific needs. The absence of emotional support from a spouse may be regretted, but single ministers may have more opportunity to find support in other areas.

Homosexuals

Men and women, but especially men, who are homosexual are very vulnerable, and may get caught up in the present anti-homosexual climate. This is not the place to debate whether homosexuals should be allowed to minister in the church or not. The simple fact is that there are many who are already there, and the church has a responsibility to care for them as people as well as ministers. Subjecting people to suspicion and investigation in their personal lives cannot be other than stressful, especially when their jobs are at risk and with the additional fear that they may end up on the front page of a tabloid newspaper. If people are to be dismissed, the church has a responsibility to do so in as caring a way as possible and to ensure that it does not treat its employees worse than most secular employers do.

Many single ministers now face extra scrutiny, extra problems in forming close friendships for fear of being misunderstood, extra worries as to whom they may confide in and extra secrecy as they try to establish their own sexual identity. All this will increase the sense of isolation, and cut them off from the very support they need and should be encouraged to seek. We risk leaving many vulnerable people very hurt. It is ironic that with the drive to minister in the inner-cities single ministers have beome very much in demand, as families are often under pressure in those situations.

Tough ministries

This brings us to the group of ministers who are seeking to serve in areas which are known to be especially tough in one way or another. It is becoming recognised that people 'burn out' very quickly in inner-city ministries. This either means that we should be thinking of short, fixed terms, or that we need to offer people in such situations much more support. This may mean team-ministries; closer supervision; support in terms of resources; more opportunities to take breaks; people willing to be called on to help in practical ways, and ready access to counselling services. It is financially foolish as well as uncaring to throw people unprepared into tough jobs and wonder why they do not survive.

Illness and disability

Major illness or disability within the family can be a source of stress which is hidden from public view. Short-term illnesses are often met with a good deal of sympathy and practical help. But it soon runs out in the face of long-term disability; the family may be thrown back on their own resources, and faced with a major drain on money, time and energy. Regular, practical help and emotional support will be much needed, and extra care when moving ministers who are caught up in this situation.

Mental illness, personality or behavioural problems tend to make people feel uncomfortable. When a minister or his children or spouse suffer from such problems, people will have even more difficulty in knowing how to respond. The family which needs extra support may well be the one which gets most isolated.

Retirement

Retirement also brings its fair share of problems. With most ministers living in tied accommodation they will have to move house. Like widows and divorcees, they may well feel that they ought to leave the area, and not get under the feet of the next minister. There is often a great call for retired ministers to take services and help out in other ways, but some do find that their change of status and role is difficult to handle. They may equally look forward to having more free time with their spouse, or for their other interests, and find themselves landed with too much responsibility during illness or interregnum.

People retiring early through ill-health face similar difficulties. A man apparently on 'the scrap-heap' in his forties or fifties feels very worthless. The church needs to find ways of enabling such people to contribute according to their skills and ability, but so often it is either 'all or nothing' in ministry, a full-time post or none at all. This is to waste both human and financial resources and there is need for much greater flexibility.

11

FINDING SUPPORT

'Social support' comprises information that leads individuals to believe that they are cared for and loved, esteemed and valued, and that they participate in a network of communication and mutual obligation.[1]

I find this a fascinating description, coming as it does from secular research. God has taken thousands of years teaching us to care, love, esteem and value each other. It is interesting to note that 'mutual obligation' is included. People are not truly supported when they are simply at the receiving end of good deeds, charity or welfare. Support involves both giving and receiving, and the vital connecting link is communication.

Research suggests that social support can protect against ill-health in the face of stress, but why should this be so? Is it a way of increasing overall wellbeing? Does having supportive people around alter your perception of how stressful a given situation is? Does support give people access to more effective ways of coping? Or is it just that stable, coping people tend to be more socially integrated as well as being better able to cope with stress? It is a difficult area in which to get hard facts because of the nature of the research required but, whatever the mechanisms, social support is certainly related in some way to both physical and mental health. This concept is not so surprising when healing is thought of as essentially something which happens *between* people. It is not something which professionals *do* to the rest of us.

Various researchers have compared groups of people with similar 'life events' scores' (see chapter three), and divided them according to whether their social support is high or low. High support groups have been shown to be less likely to have complications when giving birth, recover more rapidly from operations and TB, less likely to suffer from depression, and need less medication for asthma.

In the process of learning both to give and receive support, it is useful to divide it into different components. You may like to add some categories of your own to this list:

Emotional support is to feel valued and loved for who you are, regardless of what problems you have, or what you may have done. It is *agape* love - the human version of the unconditional love which God has for us.

Companionship is feeling that you belong and can relax and enjoy yourself with a person or group of friends; it is friendship with people you might want to spend an evening with, or enjoy a particular leisure activity together.

Listening. We all need someone who will simply listen without trying to give lots of advice or criticise what we may feel or think. The listener need only show interest and concern in us as individuals; he can be a stranger on the train or a Samaritan on the telephone, as well as someone we know well.

Practical support is knowing that you have people to call upon for help with practical things, especially during a crisis or busy period. It is not the sort of support which entails a hidden 'now you owe me something'.

Technical support comes from someone you trust to evaluate you or your work honestly and objectively, without a hidden agenda or any axe to grind. It is someone who will affirm and encourage you, but at the same time provide constructive criticisms and challenges to enable you to improve and grow.

Spiritual support is from someone with whom you can share the joys and difficulties of your spiritual journey, whom you trust enough to share things with at the deepest level, who will give you honest advice with your best interests at heart.

It was mentioned in chapter eight that most ministers feel that they receive most of their support and encouragement from their spouses. In one way this is encouraging as it reflects the strength of their marriages, but it is of concern because it also reflects on the low level of support that ministers receive from elsewhere. They are given the subtle expectation that somehow most of their support should come from within the family, and if it does not the marriage or the family is failing. But with the tendency towards the nuclear-family model, there can be a great build-up of tension within this small system. Looking at the above list, it can be seen that the general term 'support' covers many aspects. Recognition of this can save the unhappiness that results from looking for the wrong thing in the wrong place.

Michael unconsciously expected his wife, Margaret, to fulfil all six supportive functions single-handed. He felt very let down because she was unable to meet all his needs; so he blamed her for being unsupportive. On looking at things more carefully, Michael realised that she was in fact offering him very good emotional support and companionship, which he needed and valued. What he was lacking was practical support in his ministry, and someone with whom he could discuss and develop spiritually. He was put in touch with a spiritual director, and this also enabled him to feel much more fulfilled in his work. Even though he is still without the practical help he needs, he and Margaret are much happier together and much more able to appreciate what the other can give.

Single ministers, especially women, can feel very unsupported because they are more likely to be lonely and miss the intimacy of a single close relationship. They need particularly to assess which areas of support they are receiving, which they need to seek, and where it is appropriate to look.

Although ministers do spend much of their lives with people it is easy to end up lonely. This is partly because the relationships are all in one direction. People come to the minister's house wanting all sorts of things, but not straight friendship.

It is very difficult to admit to being lonely. Ministers do not want to damage their image as being permanently available to meet people's demands. But if we are lonely, it is important to admit it, at least to ourselves. To avoid doing so is to run away from our need for support and friendship, and we may then try to manoeuvre people into fulfilling that need - usually under the pretence of helping them. Peter Levin,[2] in his book *Being Friends*, quotes research suggesting that men generally have fewer and less intimate friendships than women. Indeed up to 50% of men have no one person in whom they feel that they can confide. Their only friends are work colleagues, who tend to offer companionship rather than the emotional support of true friendship. The competitiveness among ministers is not fertile ground for the growth of real supportive friendships. Seeking friendship is not easy within the local church through fear of appearing partisan, but many ministers do manage to form lasting friendships there. It is therefore important to nurture existing friendships, perhaps those we have from before entering the ministry, or from college or old family friends. Mobility and busyness mean that many such friendships tend to drift unless there is a particular commitment to nurture them.

Spiritual support may be sought in various ways, such as a spiritual director, a soul friend, or a prayer-partner. Spirituality is a very vulnerable area in which a minister may ask for help. If you are shy about approaching people you know, then a religious order or one of the newer communities may be a good place to start. Or ask colleagues or superiors to see if there is anyone they can recommend. These sorts of support systems are best set up when things are going smoothly, both because they serve to prevent future problems and because help is near at hand should problems arise.

Practical support is a perennial problem for ministers in parish work. There has been an increase in 'professionalism' among ministers during the last century or so, and we are now reaping the consequences. Church people tend to think that ministry is something only professional ministers do, and there are still a great number of churches who have a 'vicar does everything' mentality. Fred moved into one such church and spent years teaching the people to minister to each other, rather than expect that he should always be there. When he had a nervous breakdown, after a period of great family stress, he was surprised and moved to find that same caring ministry being offered to him.

Attitudes do change, but often slowly. One step is to ask for help when we need it, and find ways of making sure people know that it is appreciated when offered. It is very painful to ask for help and not receive it, and it becomes all too easy to put up the walls of defiant self-sufficiency; unfortunately that just perpetuates the problem.

There are some specialised support systems for ministers being developed. Some are based on small groups regularly meeting together around a common study or leisure interest, and others are based on a one-to-one work consultancy. These serve a different purpose from counselling services which are geared more to crisis-intervention than ongoing support. Find out what is already going on in your area, or find a respected colleague, superior or lay person with whom you can discuss things regularly. It is best not to wait for urgent problems to appear before you get your support networks organised.

12

LEARNING TO COPE

A dictionary definition of 'to cope with' is, 'to contend on equal terms with, to keep level with'. It strikes me as a very good definition of what we are trying to do with stress. Stress is here to stay. We cannot eliminate it, even if that were desirable, but we can contend on equal terms with it, keep up with it, not allow it to suffocate us. This chapter looks at some of the mechanisms we commonly use to cope. Some of them are good in some situations and counter-productive in others. Some work very well in the short-term, but the long-term cost is too high. By having a better understanding of what is going on, we can use these skills to our best advantage.

Coping includes any response to external stresses which serves to prevent, avoid or control emotional distress.[1] The three main groups are:

1. Responses aimed at minimising the discomfort experienced, rather than solving the problem
2. Responses that control the meaning of the problem after the external event, but before the stress is experienced
3. Responses that modify the situation

Minimising discomfort
Responses which minimise the discomfort experienced without changing the situation include denial, passive acceptance, withdrawal and faith (i.e. 'It's God's will'). There is a time and a place for faith in the form of passive acceptance, as in the old prayer: 'God grant me the serenity to accept the things that I cannot change, courage to change the things that I can, and wisdom to know the difference.' But sometimes 'faith' can be an avoidance of issues with which one should deal constructively.

Denial can be a very effective form of coping. Convince

70

yourself something is not really happening and the attendant distress is reduced. This is appropriate and even necessary in some situations. But it can be disastrous in others! During the initial stages of bereavement, denial is an important defence-mechanism, enabling people to cope until they are able to allow the full impact of loss to sink in. Research in Northern Ireland suggests that people who actually believe that the troubles are not as bad as they are, suffer less anxiety, tension and other stress symptoms than those with a more objective and accurate view. But denial has its problems. One, if your world view differs too much from those around you, you may risk being classed as insane! Second, and more importantly, denial of a problem means you are unlikely to do anything constructive about it. So it has its uses as an emergency coping mechanism, but it is very seldom that there is absolutely nothing you can do about a situation, not even pray?

Controlling the meaning
Responses concerned with controlling the meaning of the problem, rather than the problem itself, are an interesting and well tried group. One approach is to make positive comparisons, such as 'It could be worse'; 'There are always others worse off than us'; 'Count your blessings'. Another is to alter the values and goals. Low salary as a stressor can be minimised by substituting the rewards of job satisfaction for those of pay, or by devaluing money relative to other things.

Modifying the situation
Responses which aim to modify the situation are often most effective in situations involving relationships - negotiating, getting involved, being committed, and reflecting with others on problems. People often avoid these responses, possibly for the following reasons:
    1. The person must recognise the situation as being the source of their distress
    2. They must have some ideas on how to change the situation
    3. There is the risk that intervention may fail to change the situation, or even create another stressful situation in its place

71

It can be very useful to talk things through with a third party in order to shed fresh light on a problem and open up the 'no go' areas which often develop within relationships.

Problems which involve organisational structures and more material issues are generally more difficult to cope with than those with relationships. In these cases, who you are can be more important than what you do. They bring us back to the 'commitment, control and challenge' outlook. Even if the situation is not changed, you will be more able to cope with it by developing these qualities.

Hopelessness

Hopelessness and helplessness are signs of failure to cope. This can occur either because the problems are so overwhelming or because the person's repertoire of coping-mechanisms is inadequate. People in either situation tend to withdraw into themselves or into insanity, because they can see no alternative. People who feel helpless or hopeless are at risk, and they are very much in need of other people's support to enable them to regain a sense of their own worth and a feeling of control. It is a danger sign which superiors and colleagues need to watch out for, not least because such people may be far less 'difficult' than the ones who respond to stress by becoming awkward. When dealing with trouble-makers, it is always important to ask why their behaviour has arisen? The majority of ministers are not difficult for the sake of being difficult. When they are, it is often because they are in a corner, under pressure, unsupported, feeling that if they do not fight for their health and sanity no one else will.

Controlling the symptoms of stress

Very popular methods of coping are aimed at controlling the unpleasant symptoms of tension and anxiety. They include the use of: alcohol, nicotine, caffeine, tranquillisers and other mood-altering drugs. They work, but at a cost.

Alcohol is one of the oldest relaxants known to man, and is indeed very effective at reducing anxiety levels. At its most basic, alcohol is an anaesthetic. It appears to be a mood raiser at social gatherings, but in fact it merely accentuates the existing predominant mood: if you drink when you are feeling down, it will make you feel even more depressed, hence the danger of drinking alone to drown your sorrows. Excessive drinking and alcohol-dependence are often responses to stress, but ministers in this predicament are unlikely to get much sympathy. Colleagues and doctors are more likely to turn a blind eye to the warning signs in a minister than with other people, and many get help too late.

'Alcoholism' is a very loose term which covers a variety of potential problems with alcohol:

1. Excessive consumption (i.e. weekly intake above a specified amount)

2. Alcohol-related disability (i.e. mental, physical or social harm caused by excessive consumption)

3. Problem-drinking (i.e. that which incurs alcohol-related disability, but without dependence)

4. Alcohol dependence (i.e. mental or physical disturbance if alcohol is withheld).

Alcohol is poisonous to both the liver and brain. Regularly drinking over 35 units per week (especially if it is in binges) is damaging to your long-term health. (One unit of alcohol is half a pint of beer, one glass of wine, or one measure of spirits.) Up to 15 units per week is probably safe, and may even be good for you. But even at low levels of consumption your performance is impaired at the same time as confidence in your performance is increased. This is why someone within the legal limit of blood alcohol is twice as likely to have a car accident as someone with no alcohol at all. Once you have drunk enough to raise your blood-level to the legal limit (as little as two-to-four units) there is nothing that can be done other than giving time to reduce it. (The body clears alcohol at the rate of about one unit per hour.) The syndrome of alcohol-dependence can be a subtle one. Below are six pointers to dependence, which are a better guide than just the quantity consumed:

1. Feelings of being compelled to drink. Craving to have a drink, and knowing that once you start, you may not be able to stop.

2. Stereotyped pattern of drinking, and regular drinking to avoid withdrawal symptoms.

3. Drinking takes priority over other activities, including health, family, home, work and social life.

4. Increasing tolerance of alcohol is a sign of increasing dependence.

5. Repeated withdrawal symptoms, i.e. shakes, agitation, nausea and sweating, which often occur on waking and are relieved by drinking.

6. Relief drinking, i.e. drinking to stave off withdrawal symptoms, especially in the morning, and increasing secrecy about drinking.

Because the catalogue of physical, mental and social problems of drink is so distressing, it is vital that warning signs are heeded. Ministers are not immune from running into problems with alcohol but, as with relationship problems, the fear of censure is a powerful disincentive to seeking early help. If you think you have a problem, seek advice.

Nicotine is unique as a tranquilliser in that it improves alertness and concentration at the same time as promoting feelings of calm and relaxation. No wonder people get hooked! The effects are much the same whether the tobacco is smoked, chewed or snuffed.

The hazards are the well-known direct effects of smoke, tar and carbon monoxide on the lungs, but also the release of adrenaline. The combination means that the heart is goaded into pumping harder and faster at the same time as its available oxygen is reduced. Everybody knows that smoking is bad for you, so I do not intend to add to that guilt here. Do not be pressurised into giving up when you are already very down. Start by dealing with other areas, such as overwork and support, and if you are lucky you may find your need for nicotine as an aid to coping is reduced. If not, at least you will be much better prepared to cope with giving it up.

Caffeine is so widely used now that it is hard to imagine that it was once as illicit a drug as cocaine is today. It is found in coffee, tea, cola drinks and chocolate, as well as being hidden in some paracetamol preparations. The effect of caffeine is to increase your reactivity to stimulation, especially if you are already a 'Type A' person, and thus help keep arousal levels high. This is fine if you are on the up-slope of the human function curve, and want a boost of energy for some special effort. The only penalty is sleep disturbance, because it takes six hours for the caffeine in one cup of coffee to drop to just half of the original level. The main danger is that if you are already on the down-slope of exhaustion, caffeine means pushing the body to use reserves of energy which are already dangerously low.

If you drink coffee regularly (over four cups a day) your arousal level is permanently raised. This leaves you with little extra reserve capacity for when you really need it. Try to adapt to the pace of your natural energy levels, like a marathon runner setting a pace he can keep up for many miles. Recognise caffeine as a drug, and use it with respect. If you do drink a lot, expect your body to need time to readjust if you cut down and, as with anything else, choose a time when you are not already under undue pressure. Decaffeinated coffee is readily available, so shop around until you find a brand you like. Tea contains about half the caffeine of coffee. Luaka produce a decaffeinated ceylon tea, available from health food shops, and Rooiboos (red bush) tea also tastes reasonably like ordinary tea. Alternatively, you may like to try some of the herbal teas which are now available.

Tranquillisers and sleeping tablets have been very widely prescribed and used over the last twenty years or so. Although problems were recognised quite early on, it is only now that people are becoming more widely aware of the dangers of the group of drugs known as the Benzodiazepines. There are dozens of trade and generic names for these drugs, but some of the more familiar ones are Valium, Librium, Tranxene, and Mogadon. They are all good anxiolytics (reduce anxiety) and hypnotics (promote sleep). It is simply the relative potency of these two effects, plus the length of time the drug stays in the blood, which determines whether it is used as a tranquilliser or a sleeping pill. In either case, they should never be used for more than a few weeks at a time. People very rapidly become addicted, and withdrawal symptoms mimic the very anxiety or insomnia for which they were originally prescribed. Common side-effects are drowsiness and lethargy, the ability to drive is affected, and there can be major problems with personality change and 'emotional anaesthesia'.

These drugs really cannot be considered a substitute for human support, a balanced lifestyle and more effective ways of coping with stress. It is a tragedy and a disgrace that so many have fallen victim to their effects. Legitimate uses of the benzodiazepines include:

1. Sedation before an operation or other short-term trauma.

2. Intermittent use (one or two nights per week) as a sleeping pill for someone with long-term sleep disturbance due to intractible pain.

3. To promote a period of complete rest for someone who is exhausted, but too aroused to be able to sleep.

I think it is also fair to include *Pain-killers* in this list of coping mechanisms. Now that attention is being drawn to the hazards of the benzodiazepines, the advertising of pain-killers is changing in a worrying way. Aspirin or paracetamol advertisements now seductively suggest that the frantic housewife or busy executive can escape from the maelstrom of life into peace and tranquillity by just 'popping' a little pill; this is exactly the same type of advertising which was used to promote the benzodiazepines just a few years ago. Although they are freely available, aspirin and paracetamol are not safe drugs. If they were coming new to the market today, they would not pass existing safety standards in the light of their effects on the intestines, hearing, balance, blood clotting, liver and kidney functions. By all means use them for the occasional headache at an inconvenient time, but if you find yourself getting tension-headaches most days your body is trying to tell you something. Listen to it!

13

RELAXATION

Basic relaxation techniques are a very useful tool in one's stress-reduction repertoire. Being able to relax is an important antidote to the effects of prolonged effort. As we discussed before, the level of adrenaline production is actually decreased to below base-line levels by mental feelings of calmness and equanimity. The problem is that when you have a lot of adrenaline in your blood-stream, relaxing is the last thing you feel like doing. Even if you sit down you may feel restless and fidgety, your thoughts are racing around with anything but calmness and equanimity, and the cycle of adrenaline production is perpetuated. The way to break the cycle is to train your body to relax. Even though it may be difficult at first, after a little practice your brain gets reprogrammed, which makes it easier to relax whenever you want to.

Can you remember the last time you felt completely relaxed? If you have been busy or under pressure for months or even years, it is quite likely that you cannot! If this is the case, you may well benefit from a massage before you start which will remind your body what relaxation feels like. There are some suggestions in the chapter on massage (p. 82) on how to go about this, but if you do not have the opportunity then do not worry. Get on with learning relaxation, and allow yourself a little extra time to get the hang of it.

Physical benefits of relaxation
An American doctor, Herbert Benson,[1] has studied in detail what he calls the 'relaxation response'. He studied all sorts of people meditating, including Christian religious, Buddhist monks and practitioners of transcendental meditation and he found that the physical response was always very similar.

The rate of adrenaline and noradrenaline secretion decreases, and at the same time the body also becomes less responsive to these hormones in the blood. In other words, for the same hormone level there is a reduced effect on the body. There are also many other measurable effects of relaxation. The heart-rate and the breathing-rate both slow down. Within the first few minutes the body's oxygen consumption drops by 20% (compared with only 8-10% over four to five hours when sleeping). Oxygen consumption is a rough way of measuring the metabolic activity within the body, which includes all the chemical reactions necessary for life. So, when oxygen consumption drops by one fifth, it indicates that the whole body has gone into a lower gear. Paradoxically, body temperature rises slightly, contrasting with a drop in temperature during sleep. Among Tibetan monks, the amount of snow that they can melt with their body-heat while meditating is taken as a measure of their proficiency. Personally, I prefer to relax in an armchair, and leave such heroics to the professionals! Blood-lactate levels also drop significantly during relaxation. Feelings of anxiety raise blood-lactate, and high levels in their turn promote feelings of anxiety. Again a part of the vicious cycle is being broken. Regular practice of relaxation/meditation has also been shown to reduce blood-pressure. If you regularly relax for a minimum of 10-20 minutes each day, there is a significant drop in blood-pressure which is maintained throughout a twenty-four hour period. However, this benefit is lost within a few days of stopping regular relaxation, so it is something with which you need to persevere.

Basic relaxation technique

The most interesting point that Benson discovered is that provided four basic steps are followed these physical changes occur, regardless of whether the subject feels they had a 'good' session or not. I find this news very encouraging because my relaxation sessions frequently feel as if nothing is happening; but at least this produces the motivation to persevere.

The four basic steps outlined by Benson are:

1. Find a quiet place where you will not be disturbed.
2. Make sure that your body is in a comfortable position.
3. Have a mental word, symbol or sound to dwell on.
4. Adopt a passive attitude of mind.

Finding *a quiet environment* involves taking the phone off the hook, sabotaging the door bell, and asking family not to disturb you for this time (between 10-30 minutes). It is well worth taking these preliminary steps for a number of reasons. One reason is that you will not be able completely to relax if you have half an ear for the telephone or visitors. If you are able to keep a regular time for it, people will get to know when not to call. Another is that if you do achieve a fairly deep level of relaxation you can drop your blood-pressure fairly effectively. This means that if you are startled and leap to your feet to answer the telephone, you may find yourself feeling rather dizzy.

A *comfortable position* helps to avoid the distractions of your body needing to fidget in order to become more comfortable. Sitting in an armchair with your feet squarely on the floor and your hands resting lightly in your lap is as good as any. If you find a kneeling prayer stool comfortable, then that is another option. If you lie down, there is a tendency to fall asleep. But if you are tired, there are worse things that you may do! Relaxation exercises in bed at night can help you to unwind if you have trouble getting to sleep. If you are lying down or sitting in a chair it is a good idea to have a small cushion behind your neck. (The 12" dumb-bell shaped ones are especially comfortable. They are obtainable at orthopaedic or surgical appliance shops.) The neck and shoulder muscles are often the places where most tension builds, so it is as well to make this area as comfortable as possible.

A mental *word, symbol, or sound* to dwell on. This is where the relaxation technique begins to merge with meditation and the more specifically spiritual side of the exercise. In order to achieve the relaxation response, all you need is something to focus on which is meaningful for you. Secret mantras etc are only ways of restricting access to the benefits of relaxation, either for financial gain or for making a particular religious grouping more exclusive. Use anything which you feel comfortable with, such as 'Joy and peace'; 'Come Holy Spirit'; 'Lord have mercy'; 'Peace be with you', or words of your own choosing. Some people focus most naturally on words, but others find sounds or symbols more helpful. Any music which helps you relax can be used, or choose a picture or a candle which you can either look at directly, or just keep in your mind's eye.

The *passive attitude* of mind is both the most important and the most difficult part. The essence of it is letting go of the effort factor, knowing that there is no need to try, no need to achieve, no need to 'do it right'. Most people find it impossible to achieve a blank mind, but this is not necessary. It only makes you try and push out all the unwanted thoughts which keep cropping up. This gets the effort-related adrenaline flowing again, and successfully destroys the whole object of the operation. Stray thoughts do enter your mind, sometimes for quite long periods during relaxation. Do not be worried by them, or try and shut them out or push them away. When you become aware that your concentration has wandered, simply bring your thoughts gently back to the phrase or picture on which you were originally concentrating. The thoughts can wait until later. It can be useful just to keep a pen and paper handy, so that if you do remember something vitally important while you are trying to relax, you can write it down rather than have to worry about remembering it again.

These then are the essentials of the relaxation response. If you are new to relaxation, it can be useful to have a 'tape' to listen to which takes you through the basic steps for getting your body to relax. There are some good ones available, but if you do not feel inclined to spend money you can always record one for yourself. (Appendix 3 gives a sample script which you can use or adapt. Get a friend to do it if you do not like the sound of your own voice.) Having a tape which keeps reminding you of what you are supposed to be doing helps the concentration at first, and you may find yourself going back to using it later on if you are very tense and find it difficult to unwind for any reason.

Using relaxation

Once you have got the hang of how to relax, perhaps running through the routine five or ten times, you have it as a tool to use whenever you need it. You are beginning to train yourself to be aware of tension, and you may be surprised to find how many things provoke tension. As soon as you are aware of it you can consciously drop your shoulders, make sure you are breathing with your tummy and not your chest, and just let a wave of relaxation spread outwards to your hands and feet. You can use it during difficult telephone calls or meetings, or take a few moments each time you finish a task in order to avoid carrying over the tension in an ever-increasing burden during the day.

Most of us have potent triggers which set off tension, such as ringing telephones, traffic jams, irritating voices, slamming doors or red traffic lights. If getting tense can do nothing to change the situation, you might as well save your energy for more productive worry! By using such triggers as routine calls to relax, even for a few moments, you can greatly reduce your stress levels.

Relaxation and posture

Posture is not something which immediately springs to mind when you think of relaxation, but it can be important. If you tend to get back-ache or head-aches when you have been working at your desk for any length of time, it is well worth checking how you sit. If you are using a keyboard, your chair needs to be high enough to enable you to use it without having to hunch up your shoulders to gain extra height. But for reading or writing at a desk, your chair will need to be rather lower in relation to the desk to enable you to keep a straight back. It is worth investing in a chair with adjustable heights to allow for this. Alternatively, keep your typewriter on a lower desk, or sit on some good thick books when you type. The little extra time taken in getting ready will be amply rewarded by the reduction of strain on your back, shoulders and neck.

14

MASSAGE

Touch is our very earliest means of communication. As babies we receive messages of love, comfort and security through being held and touched. This method of communication remains very important to us in adulthood, but its use becomes increasingly surrounded by embarrassment, uncertainty and taboos, particularly for men. Part of the problem may arise from a confusion of sensuality and sexuality (with the fear that any pleasurable touch is sexual and therefore taboo). However, touch can be very pleasurable, without being sexual; sensuality is to do with being fully alive, fully partaking in the present moment, delighting in the beauty and wonder of God's creation, of which our bodies are a part.

Because it reaches so deeply into our early experiences, massage can be a very powerful way of making us feel loved and cared for, at peace with ourselves and with the world, and very relaxed. Other physical benefits include improved flow of blood and tissue fluids, and the release of muscle tension. Sometimes you can get so tense that relaxation techniques alone will only touch the surface. The deeper relaxation that can be achieved with massage is both pleasurable at the time, and also helps to teach your body what relaxation feels like so that it can be more easily achieved another time. There are a growing number of courses teaching massage, and some good books with detailed instructions. This chapter gives some very basic instructions to get you started.

The first thing is to get the environment right. Choose a warm room where you will not be disturbed, perhaps with some quiet music in the background. I always prefer to massage on the floor because it is a firmer surface, and it is much easier to move around. A bed is the next best option if you do not have a proper couch. Avoid starting within an hour of a heavy meal. Both the giver and the receiver of the massage should wear loose comfortable clothing, and the giver should be in a relaxed frame of mind. If you are tense it is very easy to transmit that tension to the person you are trying to enable to relax. Part of the secret is not to be anxious about 'doing it right'. As soon as you have a basic repertoire of strokes, the most important thing is to relax and be aware of the person you are massaging. It requires not a hard concentration but a relaxed oneness.

It is important, especially for beginners, to encourage the receiver to say what feels good or what is uncomfortable. He should not have to be concerned with hurting your feelings, as the object of the operation is to give something to him. The mutuality comes by taking turns in doing the massage - while you are the giver, the receiver is expected to do nothing but receive. Giving a massage is something to enjoy and can be very relaxing in its own right. Be willing to experiment, do not be in a hurry, and do not try too hard.

To start, the receiver should lie face down with his head turned to one side and the arms down by his sides. Pillows or cushions should be used if necessary, for comfort, but avoid a large one under the head as this makes the muscles around the neck harder to get at. (A pillow under the chest can help to correct this.) The basic techniques include:

1. Gentle rocking from side to side with the palm of your hands placed firmly on the body.

2. Direct downward pressure using the palms of your hands or balls of your thumbs. Standing up you can also use the soles or balls of your feet. Use your body weight to lean with, rather than muscular effort from your arms, or you will get tired quickly.

3. Circular movements with the thumbs or heels of your hands working into the muscles. Be careful to move the skin over muscles and bones rather than moving clothing over the skin as this causes an unpleasant burning sensation.

4. Grasping and gently lifting bulky muscles between thumb and forefinger or fingers and palm.

5. Percussion (chopping) movements with the sides of your hands.

6. Firmly moving joints through their full range of movement, especially hands, wrists, feet and ankles. (This should produce a pleasant stretching sensation, but not be painful; do not do it on joints that are already painful.)

Once you are under way you will soon work out your own routine, but here is a suggested one to begin with:

1. The back. Kneel beside the receiver and use rocking, pressure, circular and percussion movements all down both sides of the spine.

2. The shoulders. Circular and grasping movements can be used fairly firmly all over these bulky muscles, and gently up the back of the neck.

3. The arms. Pressure, circular, grasping and percussion movements can be used down both arms.

4. The hands. It may feel a bit weird at first to both give and receive hand massage, but you will soon get to enjoy it. Move all the finger, hand and wrist-joints through their full range of movement, and then use your thumbs to massage into all the fleshy parts of the fingers and palms, and between all the little bones in the wrist.

5. The legs. Rock from side to side, apply gentle pressure all the way down the back of the leg with your hands, or the sole of your foot (except on the backs of the knees). Massage deeply into the large muscles of the buttocks and backs of the legs.

6. The feet. Treat these the same as the hands. You can also use the heel or ball of your foot to apply pressure to the upturned soles of the receiver. Just make sure you keep your balance with the foot that stays on the floor, and by standing relaxed and upright with your hands hanging by your side.

The receiver can now turn over onto his back.

7. The fronts of the arms and legs. To be treated in the same way as their backs.

8. The neck. Sitting behind the head, you are in a good position to massage round the back of the neck with the tips of your fingers. Be gentle, because it can be rather tender.

9. The face. In the same position, massage all over the face (with very small movements so that you do not encourage

wrinkles!). Press gently all the way round the bony surrounds of the eyes, and massage the ear lobes between your thumb and forefinger. Use the tips of your fingers and thumbs to massage vigorously all over the scalp, which is very refreshing.

When you have finished, just sit quietly for a few minutes rather than rushing off. If he is very well relaxed, the receiver may feel a little dizzy if he gets up in a hurry. Make the most of this new feeling of relaxation and well-being.

I have concentrated mainly on massage wearing clothing, because for many people this is much less anxiety-provoking, especially if they are new to it. For skin-to-skin massage you need to use an oil to lubricate your hands. A baby oil, or massage or aromatherapy oils can be bought in any chemist or speciality shops. The bottle of oil should be warmed for ten minutes in a pan of hot water before you start, and it is especially important to make sure that your hands and the room are quite warm. Because the receiver will have wet skin he will tend to get cold more easily. It is also useful to lie on a towel to make sure that the oil does not stain fabrics or furnishings, and have another towel handy to keep him warm with when you have finished, and to rub off excess oil afterwards. Much of the basic technique is similar to giving a massage clothed, but you have the added advantage of being able to use long flowing strokes over the skin, particularly on the back, which can be very soothing. Depending on the way you approach it, massage can be refreshing and invigorating or soothing and relaxing. To be invigorating one has to work faster, and use more percussion and brisk rubbing down movements. But it is still important to be sensitive and avoid hurting with rough movements.

If you have no one available to give you a massage, but you feel that this is something you could benefit from, an option would be to contact a natural health centre locally, or look in the classified section of a magazine such as *Here's Health* for a professional masseur. It can be expensive though, costing from £10 to £20 per hour. Another option is to try using some of the techniques described above on yourself. Obviously there are some areas you cannot reach, but hands, feet and neck are fairly accessible for most people. Make sure that you are in a comfortable position to start with, either sitting or lying down. Hands and feet can be massaged exactly as described above. It is also good to work at the soles of your feet either with a golf ball held in the palm of your hand, or by treading on an 18" x 1" (diameter) dowel rod. You can buy either of these for under a pound, and they can be just as effective as the classier 'footsie rollers' which can cost anything up to £15. Percussion and circular movements can be used on the legs and arms; you can also do your own face and scalp as described above. To do your neck, start by sitting up and working with the tips of all your fingers massaging all round the back of the neck. Using one hand at a time, gently pick up small chunks of muscle between the finger tips and the palm of the hand. Give it a squeeze and then let go. This can be repeated all over the back of the neck and shoulders. To finish off, lie down comfortably on your left side with a pillow under your head. Keep your right arm relaxed by your side, and use the fingers of your left hand for circular massage movements over all your shoulder muscles. As with relaxation techniques, it can be helpful to use them last thing at night so you do not take the day's tension to sleep with you.

15

EXERCISE

Exercise is important for its ability to increase the capacity of the heart to cope with effort. On one level this is obvious - if you want to be a good athlete you have to train regularly to increase your fitness. What is less obvious is that it also increases the capacity of the heart for coping with the strains of emotional effort. By exercising you are effectively raising the height of your human function curve, enabling you to continue in the healthy function section for longer before becoming fatigued.

There are also more immediate benefits from exercise. The level of adrenaline rises during exercise, but falls to a lower level afterwards, so regular exercise has the effect of an overall lowering of the adrenaline level. There is no need to worry about the rise in adrenaline during exercise, because this is using the hormone for its proper purpose - i.e. to mobilise the resources of the body for physical effort. Adrenaline is not harmful in itself, but it does have harmful effects when used inappropriately. Other benefits of regular exercise are a reduction in blood-pressure, lower blood-cholesterol, and less muscle tension. The body also increases production of its own opiates (morphine-like substances) which raise your general mood, and reduce the tendency to anxiety or depression. Exercise will even improve your sex life!

By now you are probably wondering how to make use of these wonderful benefits when either you positively detest exercise; you have not got time for it; or, being middle-aged and very unfit, you fear its effects in the light of newspaper stories about people going out jogging and dropping dead.

If you come into the first category you have my every sympathy. Ways do need to be found of making exercise positively enjoyable, or at least as painless as possible, to avoid it becoming yet another thing about which you will feel guilty not doing, or another 'effort plus distress' trap. Ask yourself what exactly it is that you do not like about exercising? Getting organised in the first place? Competitiveness? Going out of doors? Failure? Being stiff afterwards? A general feeling of lethargy?

It is useful to think these questions through in order to find something which suits you. Are you looking for companionship, or solitude? Sporting achievement, or a modicum of physical fitness? Have you thought of swimming, dancing, rowing, cycling or skating? Mike joined his local American Football team, enjoyed the companionship of the lads, and the rough and tumble on the field provided a good outlet for his aggression. John and Sylvia took up Latin American dancing on their evening off, which gave them something to enjoy together. After a while they found it was becoming one more activity crammed into a busy diary. They regularly arrived late, feeling rushed and it provided another focus of tension between them. So they talked, sorted out their priorities, and once more they were able to enjoy it in a relaxed frame of mind. Ron uses his bicycle when he goes visiting, and finds he gets much less tense at the end of the afternoon as a result of taking a little exercise between each visit. Julia bought a dog to give her regular commitment and purpose for walking.

If time is the major deterrent, is it because you put a low priority on looking after your own needs? It might be that most of the things that you enjoy in your 'time off' are not energetic. In this case the best thing to do is to try and fit exercise into your daily routine. Always take the stairs instead of the lift. Park your car at the far end of the car park. Get off the bus one stop early. Walk to the post box. Treat chores that you don't like doing (such as chopping wood or mowing the lawn) as purposeful forms of exercise. Run on the spot to get yourself warm instead of turning up the heating.

If you have become very unfit, then it is important to be sensible. There are some basic ground rules to follow:

1. Know where you are on the human function curve. If you are on the downslope, then what you need is rest, sleep, and the opportunity to get yourself back on a healthy function upslope. Exercise is an important preventative strategy, but it can be further punishment for your body if you are exhausted. Even trained athletes

can come unstuck by pushing themselves beyond their limits when exhausted.

2. Learn to listen to your body. Know when you have had enough. There are warning signs before break-down occurs. Listen to them.

The problem with the above advice is that we have lost our natural ability to listen to our bodies. We honestly do not know when enough is enough, or when our lethargy is a sign of sloth. We need to re-learn what came naturally as children, and I offer some further guidelines for that process:

1. Your general resistance is lowered when you have been sleeping badly, when you have been under strain emotionally, when you are beginning or recovering from a virus infection, or when the weather is cold. The body's capacity is not the same each day. Because you could run a mile yesterday do not assume you can do so today if circumstances are different.

2. Always do simple warm-up exercises first, such as touching your toes, swinging your arms, or jogging on the spot. Cold muscles are more liable to injury than prepared ones.

3. Do not let yourself get cold during or after the exercise, especially when out of doors in cold weather.

4. Do not cause yourself pain. A little aching or stiffness the next day is acceptable, but actual pain is a warning signal. It is your body's way of complaining when you do too much too soon; heroics achieve nothing.

5. Feel warm, break sweat, and get slightly out of breath, but do not get so much out of breath that you cannot talk.

6. Do not expect miracles over-night. Fitness takes time to lose, and it takes time to build up again.

7. If you are keen to play a competitive sport, then first take time to get yourself fit enough. Otherwise in the excitement and challenge of your match you will almost certainly overdo things.

The Canadian Air Force has developed the XBX fitness pro-grammes[1] which only take ten minutes each day, and are designed to keep their personnel in good shape, ready for any emergency. They are carefully structured programmes for men and women which gradually fit more and more into the ten minutes. They are particularly good if you do not want a large time commitment, and need guidance as to how to become fit gradually.

If you spend a lot of time sitting at a desk, movement will help your concentration and avoid building up muscle tension. This is in addition to physical fitness, and not a substitute for it. It only takes a few minutes every half hour or so. Here is a routine for you to use:

1. Stand up straight and reach your hands towards the ceiling, stretching as far up as you can. Then flop so your hands hang down towards the floor. Bob up and down a couple of times so that they reach a little lower. Stretch up, and then touch your toes five times. It does not matter if you cannot actually reach your toes, just aim to get a little lower each time.

2. Stand up straight again, and lean to one side so that your hand reaches down the side of your leg. Do this on alternate sides five times, aiming to get a little further down each time.

3. Stand up straight and swing one arm round slowly in a complete circle, five times forwards, and five times backwards. Repeat with the other arm.

4. Still standing, let your head flop forward as far as it will go, and then roll it round in a complete circle, once to the left, once to the right. The crackling sounds are signs of muscle tension and nothing to worry about. However, if you have arthritis in the neck, or any history of instability of the neck joints, it is safer to tip your head forward, then return to the upright position, tip to one side and return, tip backwards and return etc.

5. Give the back of your neck a massage with your fingers.

The whole routine only takes about two minutes and is a good investment of time.

The curious thing about tension is that we often do not actually want to get rid of it. We would rather battle on at the typewriter without a break, or curl up in bed and go to sleep all tense. To move or relax takes a *conscious* effort, and does not always seem to be the natural thing to do. It is as if you are holding on to tension for dear life, afraid that all your coping will fall apart if you let go. That is true of the emergency 'fight or flight' reaction; it is *not* true of long-term stress. The damaging cycle of long-term tension needs to be broken to give the body and mind the resources with which to cope.

CONCLUSION

Please do not go away from reading this book feeling anxious and guilty if you are not living a new, revitalised totally stress-free life. I dislike books that give a prescription, and then imply that if you fail to carry it out you only have yourself to blame for staying unwell. I have shared with you a selection of useful signposts along the road. I hope you will find them useful for your journey, and perhaps for assisting others on their journeys too. Each of us is a unique child of God; there are no universal prescriptions.

Failure is as important to healthy growth as success. We need to remain open to the unsettling influence of the Holy Spirit. We serve a God whose folly is wiser than the wisdom of men. In the words of Michel Quoist, 'The fact remains that I am a disciple of the man who died naked on the cross, crying out in his loneliness.'

Very 'together' people may seem to have cracked the problem of living with stress once for all, but for most it is an ongoing struggle. Saying 'no' is hard. There are situations where we should say 'no', but the job needs doing, and no one else will do it, so we say 'yes'. Finding time to pray is hard enough, let alone time to relax, exercise, eat properly, and spend time with family and friends.

But God is faithful. He does stretch us, surprise us, challenge us, broaden our horizons, coax us out of our ruts, continue to draw us closer to himself in love. Early death and disability are to be prevented when possible, but they are not the ultimate failure. Only God will be the judge of what we have made of our lives, and I think he will be more understanding of our circumstances than most of us believe. A minister who felt absolutely at the end of her tether told me how she said to God, 'Help! I'm going round the bend!' 'Don't worry', came the reply, 'I'm coming round there with you!'

We do have responsibilities as individuals, but the finger of guilt needs to be pointed more at our corporate failure to care for each other than our individual failures to care for ourselves.

Appendix 1
The Society of Mary and Martha

The Society of Mary and Martha is an ecumenical charity which seeks to care for Christian ministers and their families at times of stress and crisis. Although the work has been going on in a quiet way for many years, it was only officially launched in 1987 and is still developing its ministry. There are central themes which make the ministry quite special, we believe unique, but we also seek to be responsive to new needs as they arise:

1. Availability at the end of a telephone. It is sad that so much counselling has become formal, usually 'by appointment only'. The Society of Mary and Martha tries to be as accessible as possible. People can ring up and talk there and then, or arrange to meet and talk. Members of the society live on the job and do not work an office routine of nine-to-five. It can be of enormous value to people to know that someone is available, should they need them. Current members of the society are not formally trained counsellors, but people with sensitivity, experience, and an understanding of the special needs of those in the ministry. We have contacts with trained counsellors, psychotherapists and psychiatrists, to whom we can refer people for more specialised help when necessary.

2. '12,000-mile service weeks' are run several times a year. These are currently held at the Sheldon Centre, Exeter. Some people use the weeks as a preventative measure - a time of rest and relaxation, fresh air, good food and company, the analogy being a regular service to yourself, as you provide for your car. Some people come with more immediate needs, to talk with someone, to sort out pressing personal or work problems, or to have a time of recuperation if they are run down. Numbers are small, cost is kept low, the atmosphere is relaxed and friendly, and there are workshops teaching basic skills in relaxation, meditation and massage.

3. Accommodation. Unfortunately this is very limited, at least until such time as the Society procures its own permanent home base with resident community. We are very aware that people who have run into major health or personal problems often need several weeks, or even a few months to put their lives in order. The safe, unpressured context of a small community, with people readily available when needed, is ideal in these

circumstances. Churches have few, if any, such facilities for their ministers, but it is a much needed resource.

4. Resource centre. Because the society has such a wide remit, there are inevitably people whose needs we cannot immediately meet ourselves. For this reason there is a growing network of resources, both of individuals and organisations with whom we can put people in contact.

Please do not hesitate to get in touch with the Society of Mary and Martha, if you feel we can be of help in any way. Write to:

Dr Sarah Horsman,
Administrator,
c/o Sheldon,
DUNSFORD,
Exeter, EX6 7LE
Please send an SAE.

Appendix 2
Relearning how to Breathe Properly

To practise tummy breathing, lie down with a book on your tummy and another on your chest. On your first out-breath, breathe out as far as possible. You will notice that this involves flattening your tummy. If you let the next in-breath happen naturally you will see that your tummy rises. If you breathe with your chest, the front and sides of the chest rise with each in-breath, whereas with tummy breathing the chest does not need to move at all. Just spend a few minutes practising this, until you are familiar with the difference between tummy and chest breathing. Then let your breathing settle down to a regular rhythm without concentrating on it. Note where the movement is, rather than worry about its speed.

Once you are settled into a relaxed rhythm, slow it down a little, by pausing slightly after each out-breath. If you find that the exercise makes you feel breathless, it is a sign that it is worth persevering because you are overbreathing. Do not try to rush it, but practise for about ten minutes, two or three times a day for a few weeks. Once you have got the hang of doing it lying down, progress to sitting slouched; then upright in a chair; then leaning against a wall; and finally standing up straight. When your internal 'thermostat' (see p. 22) is reset to the correct carbon dioxide level, correct breathing will feel completely natural again.

Appendix 3
Sample Script for Teaching Relaxation

Before you begin to tape-record this script, sit comfortably in a chair for a few minutes and become aware of the rhythm of your breathing. It should be slow and relaxed. Try to keep this relaxed rhythm going throughout, taking a *leisurely* breath at each group of dots. Breathe more often if you need to. The whole script should take about ten minutes.

Once you are in a comfortable position . . . gradually become aware of your breathing. . . Don't try to force it . . .just observe the rise and fall of your tummy . . . Feel the breath passing in and out of your nostrils . . . In and out . . . In and out . . . Feel your arms and legs becoming heavy . . . and your body sinking deeper into the chair . . . All your cares and worries are rising up and floating away . . . just let them go . . .

Bring your attention down to your feet . . . slowly curl your toes up really tightly . . . Feel the sensation of your feet of being really tense . . . Now as you breathe out . . . slowly let go of all that tension . . . just let it go . . . Enjoy this feeling of relaxation in your feet . . . then on another outbreath . . . let go of a little more tension . . . Notice the more relaxed feel . . . enjoy it . . . savour it . . .

Now stretch your toes out in the opposite direction . . . make them tense, and tight again . . . and relax as you breathe out . . . and let go of a little more tension again on your next out breath . . . Now point your feet . . . stretch them out as far as you can . . . and relax . . . and let it go again as you next breathe out . . . And point your toes up towards your knees . . . giving a good stretch, and then let go as you breathe out . . . and again on the next breath . . . Every time you breathe out . . . just let a little more tension drain away.

Next, feel the tension along the insides of your thighs . . . as you tightly grip your knees together . . . grip as hard as you can . . . and then let go . . . and relax a bit more as you breathe out.

And now tense your buttocks very tightly together . . . and relax . . . and let go of more tension as you breathe out again . . . Check back to your feet and calves . . . make sure they are still relaxed . . . let the tension go again . . . and feel how heavy both your legs are . . . Spend a moment or two just enjoying this feeling of heaviness . . . Even if you wanted to move them it would be a huge effort . . .

Now start again with your fingers . . . make a tight fist in both hands . . . squeeze as hard as you possibly can . . . and then relax . . . and relax again . . . And then spread your fingers as wide as you can . . . give your whole hand a really good stretch . . . and relax . . . and observe the tension flowing away . . . Then bend your elbows as far as you can . . . while they are bent, be aware of how relaxed your hands are . . . observe how one part of you can be tense . . . while another part is perfectly relaxed . . . observe the difference . . . tell your body to remember this difference . . . and then straighten your arms again and relax . . .

Return for a few moments to observing your breathing . . . note how slowly and easily the breath passes in and out . . . in and out . . . in and out . . . Now your body feels almost weightless . . . it's hard to tell what position your arms and legs are in . . . Imagine yourself floating on a bed of warm air . . . Now return to focus your attention on your shoulders . . . tense them up so that your shoulders nearly touch your ears . . . feel how much tension there is there . . . tighten it up even more . . . and then let them drop down . . . and down . . . and down . . . With each breath more tension is drained away from your shoulders . . . they feel so relaxed and heavy . . . Now raise them up just a little way . . . and notice what a little bit of tension feels like . . . remember what it feels like, and then let it go again . . . breathe out all the tension in your shoulders . . . breathe it out . . . don't hold on to any of it . . . Let it all go . . .

To relax your neck, if you are lying in bed . . . lift your head up off the pillow and hold it there, feeling the tension . . . If you are in a chair let your head hang forward . . . be aware of the tension in the back of your neck . . . Hold it there for a few moments . . . be aware of the discomfort . . . and at the same time the relaxation in the rest of your body . . . and then let your head rest back . . . what a relief . . . how good that feels . . . Now recreate that tension but without moving your head at all . . . how easy it is to gather up all the tension again . . . so practise letting it go . . . breathe it away . . . tighten up again . . . and then let go . . . don't allow yourself to hold on to any tension . . . feel it just draining out of you, leaving you totally relaxed . . . You feel completely at peace with yourself . . . at peace with the world . . . at peace with God . . .

You can end the tape here or leave a pause of however long you choose, and finish with the following:

Slowly bring your awareness back to your body. . .open your eyes and become aware of your surroundings. . .stretch your arms. . .stretch your legs. . .slowly get up and move around. . .now go on with what you have to do. . .take with you this relaxed body and peaceful frame of mind.

Appendix 4
Eating Well

We get bombarded with all sorts of information and advice when it comes to food. Much of the research and publicity is sponsored by industries with vested interests, and it ends up being very difficult to know who, or what, to believe, especially when opinions seem to change so quickly. It is easy to end up thinking, 'why bother?' What we eat is important for two reasons:

1. A good diet helps put the body in good shape for dealing with stresses.

2. A poor diet is an additional stress for the body.

While drastic changes in your diet can be a nuisance, the fact remains that most of us eat a lot of rubbish. What we in the West would regard as a normal diet today, would have been regarded as distinctly abnormal for most of the world's population throughout history. While we await definitive scientific facts, I work on the belief that God has provided what is best for us in natural form.

However, recent evidence cautions that food allergy is a common problem. It can take the obvious forms such as shellfish or strawberries, which bring about clear cut reactions. But allergic reactions to very common foodstuffs like wheat, milk or yeast can give rise to less defined symptoms, such as headaches, recurrent infections, various bowel symptoms, rashes, tiredness and weight problems, among others. They are similar symptoms, in fact, to stress itself. Moreover, food allergy symptoms may become more troublesome in times of stress. The whole subject is a complex one, and there are many people offering what seem to be very over-simplistic diagnoses and treatments. If you have had problems for many years it may be worth seeking advice from someone who specialises in food allergy (but do check out their credentials first).

Here are some general guidelines which will enable you to find a diet that is good for you without being onerous. Remember that on the whole it is not individual foods which are good or bad, but the overall balance of the diet.

1. Your digestion works best when you eat in a relaxed frame of mind, eating food that you find pleasing to look at, taste and smell. If every

meal is rushed and interrupted, you should expect problems.

2. Regular meals are better than the occasional binge padded out with snacks (which invariably tend to be junk food).

3. Food kept warm for hours loses much of its nutritional value.

4. Fresh vegetables and fruit. These are important parts of the diet. They provide much of our vitamin C, fibre and complex carbohydrates. If you like sweet foods, it is better to eat sugar in its natural form in fruit. Vitamin C is best conserved by eating foods raw, or cooking by steaming. Age, soaking, cooking in water, long cooking or keeping warm, all decrease the vitamin C content. Eat fruit and vegetables which are fresh and in season as much as possible. The very best is food you grow yourself without pesticides. However, shops are increasingly stocking organically grown produce if you don't mind paying a little extra. If buying fresh is a problem, then frozen food is generally better than dried or tinned.

5. 'Brown everything'. Bran added to a diet high in refined and processed foods may help keep the bowels regular, but it probably decreases the nutritional quality of the diet because the absorption of important vitamins and minerals is blocked. It is better to eat your fibre in its natural state, in wholegrains, beans, vegetables and fruit. Brown bread, rice and pasta are readily available. Keep an eye out for 'wheatmeal' flour and bread, which is usually white flour dyed brown. Wholemeal is what you want.

6. Carbohydrates. These are starches and sugars found naturally in grains, pulses and fresh produce. Complex carbohydrates (starches) take longer to be absorbed, and therefore avoid the rapid changes in blood-sugar which are brought about by refined sugars (simple carbohydrates). Because complex carbohydrates come ready 'packaged' with fibre, it is difficult to eat too much. Brown and white sugar, molasses, syrups and honey are all refined sugars which are good for treats, but should not feature largely in your diet. White sugar has no minerals or vitamins, but the others do have some. Many brown sugars are merely white ones dyed; assume them to be such unless they say otherwise, or state a country of origin on the pack. Watch the labels on foods for unexpectedly high sugar levels, especially in soft drinks, fruit juices, breakfast cereals, tinned fruit, and savoury tinned products. Many people are using saccharin and other artificial sweetening products. The safety of these is disputed, and clear facts are not yet available. If you can temper your sweet tooth, so much the better. If not, there may be little to choose between sugar and sweeteners, but if you are over-weight you would be better off without the extra calories in sugar.

7. Fats. It is generally agreed that the average western diet is too high in fat. Weight for weight, fats contain twice as many calories as proteins or carbohydrates, so if you are trying to lose weight it is a good idea to cut down on all fats.

Most animal fats (plus coconut and palm oil) are 'saturated' fats; most vegetable oils (plus fish oils) are 'unsaturated' fats. As a rule, saturated fats are less good for you than polyunsaturated oils. The problem is that the refining processes employed with many natural oils probably means that they end up no better than saturated fats! 'Virgin' or 'cold pressed' vegetable oils come complete with their own vitamin E as anti-oxidant (to stop them going rancid). It is also believed that vitamin E helps protect against heart disease and cancer. Branded vegetable oils are chemically extracted and contain artificial anti-oxidants which are certainly not beneficial to health, and may be harmful. All oils break down at very high temperatures and can release harmful components. If you can grill or bake instead of frying, the fat content of the food will be lower. If you want to fry or deep fry, then don't overheat the oil. (Black smoke means it is too hot!) Do not re-use it more than three or four times. Even when baking cakes or pastries, it is often possible to replace fats with oils - look out for suitable recipes.

In order to make an unsaturated vegetable oil into a spreading margarine it is necessary to saturate it partially by bubbling hydrogen gas through it. This process makes compounds which are not found in nature ('trans' isomers instead of 'cis' isomers), which may be just as bad as saturated fat. The only unhydrogenated margarines on the market which I have come across are *Vitaseig* and *Vitaquell*, but they are only available in health food shops and are expensive. One alternative is to make a spread from equal quantities of butter and a cold-pressed oil in a food processor or liquidiser. I compromise by using butter (preferably unsalted or only slightly salted) when taste is important, Vitaquell as a spread when taste is less important and a cold-pressed oil (such as sunflower, safflower, corn or olive) for most cooking purposes.

8. Protein foods. Since the days of malnutrition in pre-war Britain we have been brought up to believe that protein is the most important part of the diet, and that animal protein is superior to vegetable protein. While protein is an important part of the diet, it is the one thing that most of us do get enough of these days. Animal proteins are very tasty, but do tend to come 'packaged' with a lot of fat. Even the lean meat of intensively reared animals can contain up to 30% fat. Sausages and other processed meats can be even higher, as well as containing added salt and nitrites. On

the whole, animals which had a chance to run about in life have lower levels of saturated fat than ones which have lived in cages or pens. Fish is a good animal source of protein because the fat is unsaturated. Eggs and cheese are fine in moderation, but watch the fat content.

Do not forget to make good use of proteins of vegetable origin. The only reason they are called 'second class' proteins is because they need to be eaten together in order to get all the basic protein building-blocks, which the body is unable to make. For example, beans should be combined with grains in order to make the protein complete. If you are not familiar with using these foods, treat yourself to a basic vegetarian/wholefood cook book to get you started.

9. Salt. All the salt we need comes naturally in small quantities, in almost all foods. The western diet contains ten to fifteen times more than we need, making the kidneys work much harder to keep salt and water balanced in the body. Excess salt is almost certainly a factor in causing high blood-pressure. One of the reasons we have come to have such a high intake of salt is that it is cheap, a good preservative, 'more-ish' and has a long shelf-life. So manufacturers put it in anything and everything. We are well and truly addicted! If you eat a lot of ready-prepared foods, check the labels and aim to buy from the developing range of low salt and salt-free products on the market. There is no need to add any salt in cooking, and always taste your food before adding it at the table. Our taste for salty foods is largely habit, and although you may miss it at first, you will soon no longer want such high quantities.

In summary, try and eat a good variety of foods, especially fresh foods and those of vegetable origin. Try to cut down on animal fats, refined carbohydrates and salt. Above all, enjoy it!

Appendix 5:
Practical Resources

These are suggestions to help you find what you need, not a comprehensive list. Costs are guides at 1989 levels. The Society of Mary and Martha is available as a resource centre, as well as offering a specific ministry of its own. If you have trouble finding what you need, do contact the Society of Mary and Martha, c/o Sheldon, Dunsford, Exeter EX6 7LE (0647-52203). We shall do our best to help.

Places of Retreat
There are so many religious orders, christian communities and specialised retreat houses that it is beyond the scope of this book to list them all individually. I have therefore included some useful publications to point you in the right direction. Check on cost when you write for details. Expect to pay at least the going bed-and-breakfast rate, say £10-£25 per night. However, many places do offer special rates for ministers, or have bursary funds available in special cases of need, so don't be afraid to ask.

The Vision. An ecumenical journal about retreats published annually in December by the National Retreat Centre. Available from Liddon House, 24 South Audley Street, London W1Y 5DL (01-493 3534).

Directory of Christian Groups, Communities and Networks. Published by the National Centre for Christian Communities and Networks. Available from Westhill College, Selly Oak, Birmingham B29 6LL (021-472 8079).

Out of this World. A Guide to Religious Retreats by George Target. Published by Bishopsgate Press Ltd, 37 Union Street, London SE1 1SE.

Away from it all: A guide to Retreat Houses by Geoffrey Gerard. (fourth edition, 1989.) Published by Lutterworth Press, P.O. Box 60, Cambridge CB1 2NT.

Residential Centres offering psychotherapy and healing in a Christian context.
Foundations run by Roman catholic religious orders with an ecumenical ministry. The programmes are well structured, and cater especially for priests and religious.

Heronbrook House, Sisters of Charity of St Paul, Bakers Lane,

Solihull, West Midlands B93 8PW (0564-776214).

Syon House, Vocation Sisters, Angmering, West Sussex BN16 4AG (0903-783315).

Residential Centres with a special emphasis on the Christian Ministry of Healing

The Old Rectory, Crowhurst, Battle, Sussex TN33 9AD (042483-204).

Burrswood ,Groombridge, Tunbridge Wells, Kent TN3 9PY (0892-863637).

Spennithorne Hall, Spennithorne, Leyburn, North Yorkshire DL8 5PR (0969-23233).

Christian organisations offering counselling, psychotherapy, and/or healing in a non-residential setting.

Professional rates for psychotherapy or counselling vary, but £10-£20 per hour is about average at the time of publication. Some places offer bursaries, or you may well be able to get help with fees from your own local or area church funds.

The Dympna Centre, 60 Grove End Road, London NW8 9NH (01-286 6107). For clergy, religious, and full-time church workers.

St Marylebone Healing and Counselling Centre, Marylebone Road, London NW1 5LT (01-935 6374). Churches Council for Health and Healing. Counselling, healing and befriending; available to anyone.

Westminster Pastoral Foundation, 23 Kensington Square, London W8 5HN (01-937 6956). Counselling for individual, family and marital problems. (There are also various offshoot organisations of the WPF around the country.)

Saint Anne's - A Centre for Listening, Under Down, Gloucester Road, Ledbury, Herefordshire HR8 2JE (0531-4841). Counselling and psychotherapy available to anyone.

Church Army Counselling Service, 10 Daventry Street, Marylebone, London NW1 (01-723 0573). Counselling available to anyone. (There is also a branch in Manchester.)

Catholic Marriage Advisory Council, 23 Kensington Square, London W8 5HN (01-937 3781).

Relate/Marriage Guidance see your local Yellow Pages (under Social Service and Welfare Organisation). Although not a specifically Christian organisation many of the counsellors are Christians.

Appendices

Health Care

British Holistic Medical Association, 179 Gloucester Place, London NW1 6DX (01-262 5299). Provides information on holistic health care.

St Luke's Hospital for Clergy, 14 Fitzroy Square, London W1P 6AH (01-388 4954). Free treatment for anglican clergy, families, ordinands and lay workers, especially surgery; recuperation for those unable to work through physical or nervous exhaustion. (No in-patient psychiatric care.)

With the growing popularity of alternative medicine, there are inevitably untrained people offering their services alongside *bona fide* practitioners, and it can sometimes be hard to differentiate between them. A good therapist will not be offended if you check out his qualifications and credentials first.

Natural Health Centres/Clinics are good places to start locally (under Natural in your telephone directory.)

The Institute for Complementary Medicine, 21 Portland Place, London W1N 3AF (01-636 9543). May be able to put you in touch with qualified therapists locally.

Specialist/Self-help Groups

National headquarters are given, who may be able to put you in touch with local groups. Alternatively try your local telephone directory

Bereavement: Cruse, Cruse House, 126 Sheen Road, Richmond, Surrey TW9 1UR (01-940 4818).

Depression: Fellowship of Depressives Anonymous, 36 Chestnut Avenue, Beverley, North Humberside HU17 9QU (0482-860619).

Separation/Divorce: Magdalene Fellowship, Meadow View, Rectory Lane, Fringford, Bicester, Oxon OX6 9DX (08697-8260).

Broken Rites, 8 Abbey Square, Chester CH1 2HU (0244-42526). For separated or divorced ministers' wives.

Tranquillisers: Tranx, 17 Peel Road, Harrow, Middx HA3 7QX (01-427 2065).

Alcohol: Alcoholics Anonymous, PO Box 1, Stonebow House, York YO1 2NJ (0904-644026).

National Council on Alcoholism, 3 Grosvenor Crescent, London SW1X 7EE (01-235-4182) - advice on where to seek help.

Ministry support and development

Edward King Institute for Ministry Development, 51a Wragby Road, Bardney, Lincoln LN3 5XR (0526-398075). Consultations for individuals to help them review and develop their ministry.

Ministry to Priests Programme, Centre for Human Development, 23 Kensington Square, London W8 5HN (01-937 4077). The team promotes peer support groups and individual growth and development, mainly for Roman catholic priests.

Holidays

The Church Army, Independents Road, Blackheath, London SE3 9LG (01-318 1226). Holds a list of free or cheap holidays available to ministers and their families.

Financial help

Various grant making trusts exist to offer grants direct to particular groups of ministers (mainly anglican). Write for an application form, or in emergency telephone with details of what you need.

Corporation of the Sons of the Clergy, 1 Dean Trench Street, Westminster, London SW1P 3HB (01-799 3696). Grants to anglican clergy, their widows and dependants for any finanancial problems except holidays and the purchase of property.

The Friends of the Clergy Corporation, 27 Medway Street, Westminster, London SW1P 2BD (01-222 2288). Grants to anglican clergy, their widows and dependants for any financial problems except purchase or expenses of motor vehicles and education fees. (They also have five self-catering holiday flats in Eastbourne available.)

The Mylne Trust, c/o Messrs Potter & Kempson, 11 South Street, Farnham, Surrey GU9 7QX. Supplement to income for retired Christian workers, especially missionaries and evangelists.

The Reverend Doctor George Richards Charity, c/o A.J. Williams, Croxons, Church Lane, Great Holland, Frinton-on-Sea, Essex CO13 OJS. Grants to anglican clergy unable to work through sickness. Initial application should be supported by letter from Bishop or Archdeacon

The Royal Asylum of St Ann's Society, Wormley Hill, Godalming, Surrey GU8 5SG. Grants for for Church of England school fees.

The Society for the Relief of Poor Clergymen, c/o Falcon Court, 32 Fleet Street, London EC4Y 1DB (01-353 0751). Grants for evangelical anglican clergy and their dependents. Not for education or car purchase.

NOTES

Introduction
1. Please apply (with SAE) to: Dr Sarah Horsman, Sheldon, Dunsford, Exeter, EX6 7LE

Chapter 3
1. Friedman M. and Rosenman R.H. *Type A behaviour and your heart.* (1974 London. Wildwood House)
2. Totman R. *Social causes of illness.* (1979. Souvenir Press)
3. Holmes and Rahe. *Social readjustment rating scale.* (1967): *Journal of Psychosomatic Research* (11. 213-8)
4. Kobasa S.C. *Hardiness and health; a prospective study*: (1982). *Journal of Personality and Social Psychology* (42:168-177)

Chapter 4
1. Henry J.P. 'Coronary heart disease and arousal of the adrenal cortical axis', in *Biobehavioural bases of coronary heart disease.* eds Dembroski et al. (1983. Basel:Karger 365-381). Illustration reproduced by kind permission of P. Nixon from his adaptation of of of J. P. Henry's diagram.
2. Nixon P.G.F. *The Human Function Curve.* 1976: (*The Practitioner.* 217. 765-769 and 935-944). Illustration reproduced by kind permission of Dr Nixon.
3. Nixon P.G.F. Quoted in *Stress and today's man.* by J.P. Henry. (Newspaper Publishers Handbook, 1984)

Chapter 5
1. *Job stress and burnout. Research, theory and intervention perspectives.* ed Paine W.S. (1982. Sage, Beverley Hills)
2. Quoted in Pryor R.J. *At Cross Purposes: Stress and support in the ministry of the wounded healer.* (1986, The Commission on Continuing Education for Ministry, Uniting Church in Australia, Synod of Victoria)
3. *Job stress and burnout in the Human Service Professions.* ed Farber B.A. (Pergamon Press)

Chapter 7
1. Eadie H. *The Helping Personality.* (Summer 1975. Contact 49)
2. As 5.3
3. As 5.3

Chapter 8
1. As 5.2
2. Devereux H. *Breakdown of Clergy Marriages* (1985)

Chapter 9
1. Fowler J.W. *Stages of Faith.* (1981. Harper & Row. San Francisco)
2. As 5.2
3. Jeff G.H. *Spiritual Direction for every Christian.* (1987. SPCK)

Chapter 10
1. As 5.2

Chapter 11
1. Cobb. 'Social support as a moderator of life stress'. (1976. *Psychosomatic Medicine.* 38. 300-314)
2. Levin P. *Being Friends.* (1987 Fount)

Chapter 12
1. Pearlin and Schooler. *The Structure of Coping.* (1978. *Journal of Health and Social Behaviour.* 19. March. 2-21)

Chapter 13
1. Benson H. *The Relaxation Response.* (1977. Fount)

Chapter 15
1. *The Royal Canadian Air Force XBX plan for Physical Fitness.* (1958. Penguin)